Summer Wine a

Summer Wine and Vintage Years

A Cluttered Life

Bill Owen

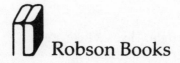

Robson Books

For Kathie

This Robson paperback edition first published in 1995

First published in Great Britain in 1994 by Robson Books Ltd, Bolsover House, 5–6 Clipstone Street, London W1P 8LE

Copyright © 1994 Bill Owen
The right of Bill Owen to be identified as the author of this work has been asserted by him in accordance with the Copyright, Designs and Patents Act 1988

British Library Cataloguing in Publication Data
A catalogue record for this title is available from the British Library

ISBN 0 86051 950 3 (hbk)
    0 86051 985 6 (pbk)

Printed in Great Britain by WBC Book Manufacturers Ltd, Bridgend, Mid-Glamorgan.

My thanks to Harry Lovelock, friend and
collaborator

Contents

Contents

Foreword by Lindsay Anderson

How often meetings which turn out to have meant a great deal to us have seemed at the time unremarkable or even mistaken. I well remember my scepticism when the casting director of the Royal Court Theatre introduced me to Bill Owen, suggesting that he should play Mr Shaw in David Storey's *In Celebration*. As Bill reminds us, it had first been my intention to cast the play with actors from the North – and he, a Londoner born and bred, had never played a Yorkshireman. But it took only a few minutes for me to be amazed by the authenticity and truth of Bill's reading, and to realize that I was in the presence of a very fine actor. So Bill became a Storey actor and went on to play the lead in two more of David's plays which I had the good fortune to direct, as well as to repeat that creation of Harry Shaw in the film of *In Celebration*, which we made with its original Royal Court cast. 'Great' is an adjective used more than once by critics writing about Bill's performance in those plays, and without doubt David's style, poetic and deeply felt as well as intelligent and often sardonic, proved exactly right for Bill, himself sometimes formidable, always caring and exceptional.

I would like to think that his perfect incarnation of the characteristic Yorkshireman in those plays had something to do with his Compo in *The Last of the Summer Wine*, the series whose fantastic and long-running success has made Bill one of

Britain's best-known and best-loved personalities. It comes as no surprise to learn that the town of Holmfirth, where those stories were shot, has found a very special place in his heart. He has spent so many years of comedy and warm-hearted eccentricity there, experiencing and giving the blessing of laughter. But perhaps it is surprising to realize, as Bill himself makes clear, that from a rather unpolitical youth, he became and remains a staunch Socialist. Of course his leftism has always been in the English style, which means passionate and pugnacious, never conformist or dry. The Socialism, in other words, of common sense. Straightforward.

A straightforward habit of thinking and expressing himself has always been Bill's way; and this is what makes his story quite unlike the usual book of theatrical reminiscences. It is, to begin with, completely honest. We learn, of course, the way he survived, through sheer doggedness, the ups and downs of this most taxing of professions. He has been a writer as well as an actor. And we learn also how the strength of his social and political convictions has given him impetus and perspective throughout his career. He calls his life 'cluttered'; I would describe it rather as always an energetic one, essentially all of a piece. It is good particularly to read from experience of the great early days of the Unity Theatre, that band of devoted brothers and sisters who did so much, before Theatre Work-shop or the Royal Court were more than a gleam in anybody's eye, to maintain and advance the cause of progressive theatre.

Though it is never insisted on, class, that favourite, in-escapable concern of the English, is a theme that runs all the way through this story. This is what underlies the undaunted progress of William John Owen Rowbotham, the little London boy of Acton Green, to Bill Owen, one of Britain's best and best-loved actors. The Rank Organization, of course, that most middle-class of respectable institutions, got him to change his name even though (he was perhaps a bit early on the scene) they never quite knew what to do with him. The Royal National Theatre has signally failed to celebrate his work;

though they've had no one like him. Still, he has had the last laugh. An acknowledged artist and a good friend, his story is a unique one. I am happy to know myself a part of it.

Lindsay Anderson

Acknowledgements

We would like to thank Roy Clarke and the BBC for the use of the pilot script of *Last of the Summer Wine*, reproduced on pages 150–56, and to the *Yorkshire Post*, the *Western Mail*, the *Tribune*, the *People*, *Punch*, the London *Evening Standard* and Times Newspapers Ltd for excerpts from their television and theatre reviews.

Introduction

CLUTTER!

'She's a regular old clutterbuck,' my mother would say when referring to someone who monopolized a conversation in which she was trying to participate. I never found a satisfactory derivation of this lovely old word, but in the many definitions of 'clutter' I came across, my favourite is 'Interfering echoes on a radar screen caused by reflections from objects other than the target'. So Mother was right ... but when wasn't she? A clutterbuck for her was the perpetrator of a shotblast of unguided words – or missiles – that usually failed to find their target. Well, in my attempt to record a cluttered life, I have inescapably fallen foul of the 'clutterbuck effect', but I hope even so the reader's appetite is and remains whetted.

My difficulty was keeping a grip on the storyline, such as it was, for ideas would bounce off one another until the order of things had flown out of the window. Memories were invoked by coincidence or circumstance. For instance, I heard of my father's death as I was being led around the parade ring at Newmarket on a horse called Bountiful during the making of the film *The Rainbow Jacket*. And then a lifetime later Compo was voted the scruffiest character on TV. This reminded me of filming in a field and being caught in a downpour, whereupon I snatched an old waterproof from a nearby scarecrow. (The farmer subsequently charged me a tenner for it!) I wore that coat, as Compo, for years. Eventually it was stolen – by the scarecrow, perhaps? Then my mind drifted to our first digs whilst filming for the pilot slot of *Last of the Summer Wine* on Comedy Playhouse. The pub was situated in the valley off the road to Marsden in Yorkshire and as I ordered some drinks I noticed a handwritten sign: 'Try our Sunday morning breakfast – with Strippers. All off!' At first having only glanced at it I wondered what was so special about Sunday morning breakfast with kippers? When I read a second time my imagination ran riot. Of course, as Jimmy Gilbert, our producer, pointed out, it may have meant that Strippers were off the menu for Sunday breakfast. But whatever, such delights were never to be ours – we returned home on the Friday.

Before proceeding further, I must scotch any ideas about this being some kind of planned Prologue, written before settling in front of the typewriter to write the book proper. In fact I am writing this weeks after handing the completed manuscript on to my long-suffering agent and pal. A beautiful friendship almost foundered when I called down the phone, 'Hold everything!' His reply, concise, articulate and very much to the point, I don't intend repeating here. But, as I explained, there are things that have to be mentioned before putting the lid on the Olivetti. 'For instance?' he asked. Well, like my eightieth birthday party where I was told about the possibility of *Summer Wine* being included in the *Guinness Book of Records* as the longest-running comedy series in the world. Also there was the advice given to me by some erstwhile publisher and wiseacre who pontificated, 'Whatever you do, don't let the book develop into a catalogue of your acting career, that sort of thing can become very boring to the reader.' I then asked him what other reason I could have for writing the book? I had no illusions that despite my long and varied career, the only reason I was being asked for my autobiography was because I brought to life an aged little clown called Compo. Mentioning his name was enough to make children smile; a national figure who reflects more adulation than I have known before in my life. 'No question,' he agreed. 'But they still like a bit of scandal; beef it up a little.' Well, I read somewhere that there is no such thing as an honest autobiography. How can any of us be sure that our childhood images, seventy-odd years on, are authentic? Take my Uncle Ernie who I met but once as a wee boy – how is it that after all these years I retain such a clear picture of him? Or do I? Have I, because of one overriding characteristic of his, re-invented the remaining memory of him? Thus he remains strong in my mind, even today. Conversations, too, like well-worn tapes, have been re-played and in many cases reinforced with an actor's and writer's imagination. I have also discovered in the course of putting this book together that my memory serves me best when recalling events outside my acting career. There have been so many films, so many plays, so many actors whose company I have enjoyed – for the run of the play. With the exception of Freda and Ian Shand there has never been another lasting professional friendship. If truth be known, we actors are like ships that pass in the night.

Well, after all that clutter I've almost talked myself off the 'radar screen'! But before I send the 'curtain up' I must mention that I have my dear mother to thank for secretly keeping a scrapbook of my press cuttings, photographs, programmes, etc., recording my amateur and early professional endeavours – which have been added to by the three other most important women in my life. The albums, recording my 57 years as a professional entertainer, number more than a dozen, some of tome-like proportions, and without them, to serve as reminders and points of reference, this might have been a very short story. So to begin at the beginning . . .

1

A Preordained Life

People, rather than places, have been the real milestones in my life and if I have difficulty in segregating the first and most important influences it is because I loved all three equally, each one playing a significant role in my formative years.

My father's name was William George Davenport Rowbotham and I remember, as a small boy, being impressed by the name Davenport. It was a name entirely foreign to me, even to this day I might add, and certainly to the residents of Acton Green, London W4, where I spent most of my childhood. On my birth certificate his occupation is given as 'Commercial Clerk'.

Within months of my birth the Great War of 1914–18 was declared and he volunteered to become one of the 'Lions led by Donkeys' thrown into that useless carnage of human sacrifice. I, naturally, have little memory of him during those early years, other than a few sepia photographs passed on to me by my mother; probably taken when he was home on leave, and I remember a certain pride in seeing him in his Quartermaster-Sergeant's uniform. With the signing of the Armistice he was posted further afield, documenting the return of allied troops to their homeland. I still have one of the souvenirs he brought back from India, an elephant carved in ebony. There were others, a pair of vases from Japan, a model of a Greek soldier, and a pair of Turkish slippers covered in

1

elaborate needlework. These were solid evidence of his travels, sitting on the mantelpiece in the front room, regularly dusted and to be replaced in exactly the same position; conversation pieces for visiting relatives invited for a Sunday-afternoon winkles-and-watercress tea.

My mother was not so well served with Christian names. She is registered on my birth certificate as just Louise, who gave birth on 14 March 1914 to a son tipping the scales at 14 pounds, christened William John Owen Rowbotham and determined to scream non-stop for the first two months of his life. This was due, it was later discovered, to an aversion to breast feeding. The story goes that my granny, whose authority has to be taken seriously regarding such matters, she being the local midwife, prescribed diluted condensed milk. Of course, the options for curing any ailment, including serious illness, were far more limited than the 'miracles' of medical science and surgery available today – or should be available, if only we had governments that saw the nation's health as a moral right rather than an economic problem. In those days there was, of course, that magic potion of varying colours prescribed by the pre NHS 'panel doctor' in whom we pinned our faith.

But back to the saga of the condensed milk. It worked so well that I slept and slept *and* slept; so much so that my mother, in a panic, woke me in fear that I might have expired! That was also, so story has it, the first time I smiled. This became a family legend told by both my mother and Granny at the same time and at the drop of a hat. It haunted me until I was well into my teens.

The war over, this stranger whom I'd been told to call 'Daddy' came back to live with us; he would soon prove to be the greatest and dearest friend I ever had. However, Lloyd George's 'fit country for heroes to live in' proved, as usual, to be nothing more than the fine words of braying politicians – the reality was unemployment and the dole queue.

Our home was a small three-roomed flat with a cold-water wash-house and lavatory. My parents slept in one room,

Granny and I in another, the third was used for every other purpose and activity. The flat was located in what was known locally as the 'poor end' of Bridgeman Road, no doubt due to the fact that it was only a footbridge that separated us from the then dire slums of South Acton.

The bedroom I shared with my grandmother was a place of many secrets – mine and hers. Why did she sob every night for weeks when my Uncle Sydney died? This depth of sorrow was very frightening to me and I pulled the eiderdown over my head to blot out the sadness. Where he'd come from I never knew. He was suddenly there, asleep on the sofa, and the rota of ablutions became more complicated – a bonus for me which sometimes gave me the opportunity to slip off to school unwashed. Within a few months he was dead from tuberculosis, or as it was then known, 'consumption'. I was intrigued by him, but could never understand why he looked so different from the other aunts and uncles on my mother's side of the family. Swarthy complexioned, extremely handsome, he looked just like Rudolph Valentino. It was some forty years later when sitting with my mother, making family gossip, that I asked about Uncle Sydney. This evoked a single comment – 'He was born on the wrong side of the blanket!'

I am always amazed how childhood memories remain so firmly focused, while someone I met yesterday can already be fading into non-existence. Sunday afternoons in winter, when for this small boy, the world seemed to stand still, all quiet except for Mr Monkton with his horse and cart, exhorting us to partake of his delicacies – 'Come and get yer whelks, shrimps and mussels – all alive-o!' Why do I always associate him with the joy and warmth of my mother, comforting me during a zeppelin raid, huddled together under a table in the darkness?

A child's toy as simple as a wooden scooter is a rare thing in this age of high technology, but the sight of one immediately brings to mind a gleaming machine of polished wood, red-plated wheels and a ringing bell that my father brought, as if by magic, from behind our never-played, out-of-tune, upright piano. That birthday morning I was up and dressed, waiting expectantly in the kitchen, listening for some sign of life from the grown-ups. Suddenly my mother appeared in her nightdress and led me into the front room to watch this loving ceremony. Of course, I had to ride it immediately, but it was still dark and Dad stood freezing at the front gate as I careered up and down outside the house. 'Not so fast, not so fast!' he called. I wonder how much penny-pinching and sacrifice went into the purchase of what was the first and one of the very few birthday presents that I remember?

I also recall the night my mother took me into our next-door neighbours' flat. It was a visit more out of sympathy, than friendship. There had been a great deal of noise coming from their flat, as was usual when the husband came home drunk; mostly raised voices as they rowed, then suddenly, thankfully, all would be quiet which meant he had staggered off to bed. But that night had been particularly violent and my mother, perhaps sensing a call for help, felt she had to go; because my father was at a meeting and my grandmother out delivering some poor mite into the world, my mother had no option but to take me with her.

I stood clutching her hand as I looked around the room where everything seemed to be broken. A wardrobe lay on its side, its door hanging off its hinges. The mirror was smashed and cast a hundred reflections from a single gas mantle. My mother did her best to console the woman. Why such needless destruction? Why? But there was no blame laid against the husband. Tomorrow he would work on his tiny patch of garden, silent until it was dark. And my grandmother would say, 'Shame, that's what he's got, shame.' For months there would be peace, but everyone knew he would do it again, sometime.

A few years later my mother and I watched from our front-room window as a coffin was carried to a horse-drawn hearse and that same woman with her three children clambered into the waiting carriage. As the sad cortège moved off, my mother said, 'Ah, well, she'll have a bit of peace now.'

We do not seem to have been a family for memorabilia. I never discovered a photograph album or even holiday snapshots, but then we couldn't afford holidays in those days. However, there were exceptions, particularly in my case. Whatever the sacrifice, ways and means were found to get 'Little Billy' to the country or the seaside. Unsuspecting relatives, no matter how distant, living in such places were wooed by either Mother or Granny in order to win their hospitality for William junior. Even my father entered into this scheme of things. Whilst serving as a senior NCO with the Territorial Army he managed to smuggle me into their summer camp at Littlehampton. And I do mean smuggle! I could have been no more than five or six years old, but I still have clear memories of being passed overhead from one giant pair of hands to another, to be hidden under carriage seats or on luggage racks during routine inspections.

But my most memorable holiday was the one I spent just outside Waltham Cross, which today is but a mere suburb of London, but seventy-four years ago when it could only be reached by steam train from King's Cross or tram from the terminus at Caledonian Road, the journey was for me an adventure in itself. Grandma had rekindled an almost non-existent relationship with a nephew who ran a small market garden. She tactfully broached the subject of my spending a holiday with him and his family and they welcomed me with open arms.

It was a wearying walk from the station that eventually took us out of town and along a leafy lane where my mother and Grandma finally came to a halt to stare somewhat dismayed at a small tumbledown house set in an acre or so of vegetables and greenhouses. But I had run on excitedly to the front gate where there was a great cacophony of welcoming sound from the chickens, geese, piglets, dogs, cats – and a donkey. Suddenly a jolly woman with a round face like a rosy apple, with figure to match, came forward to greet us.

Clara laughed a lot, it was a habit of hers and seemingly one that her children shared as they chased excitedly around us, sitting on the tired sofa set amidst the chaos of the kitchen. I was ignored by the three women, who gossiped furiously until the kettle began to boil for tea, when Clara went to the back door and with a voice like a foghorn called her husband.

My first impression of Uncle Ernie is the only one I can recall. The reason for this is that during my entire two-week stay he never changed his clothes. I began to wonder if he slept in them. There was a permanent hue of green about him, no doubt due to his being in constant contact with his tomato plants. His greasy cap, I was sure, was part of his head, an old shirt open to the navel exposed a barrel-like belly that overflowed a pair of trousers that stayed up as if by magic. But he was a gentle giant of a man, somewhat shy in the presence of the two strange women. Grandma had delivered him as a baby but he had not met my mother before. Picking me up like a feather and holding me high he exclaimed, 'Don't worry, we'll look arter li'l Bill.'

Having drunk his tea he made to leave, but as he paused at the door he farted. My mother went as red as a beetroot, Grandma coughed and pretended it had not happened. But the rest of the family took no notice whatsoever, in fact *they* did it all the time. I can't vouch for the animals, but for me that was to prove to be the great fascination of the holiday – the freedom to fart!

You see, even as a small boy I had been taught that if by accident even the mildest 'poop' were to escape, I was to say 'pardon'. This was quite understandable as far as the Rowbotham family were concerned; we were four human beings trying to exist in our cramped home in Bridgeman Road and certainly no place for the maxim 'Wherever thou be, let thy wind flow free'. But I shall never forget wandering through the tomato plants with Uncle Ernie when he suddenly produced what sounded like the entire percussion section of the 1812 Overture – including cannon. I often tried to match his performance when alone among the tomatoes – until I, shall we say, overreached myself with unforgettable results!

Despite the family's seeming reluctance to leave any record of a family tree, I discovered to my great surprise, among my mother's few effects, three studio portraits, one of which showed me as a bonny baby, naked on the inevitable rug. They were all posed and formally taken by, as is shown on the back of each photograph, Mr George Morgan at his 'Daylight and Electric Light Studio' at 215 The Grove, Hammersmith, London W6, where, my mother had told me years earlier, if the portrait was considered good enough – and the customer likewise – you might have the honour of being 'hung' for all to see in his private arcade. So it became the local point of attention for the family Rowbotham when out for their Sunday afternoon stroll. But – there was a hint of sadness in my mother's voice as she finally closed the subject – 'But we were never hung.'

Other memories of those early days ... inevitably, the fascination of sex and at an early age – or so it seemed in my case. First, the innocent inquisitiveness under the pretext of playing 'doctors' and rummaging around Nellie Price's anatomy. She was the big girl who lived in the downstairs flat. There was also my quasi-sexual experience with May Turner, the pubescent Gypsy Rose Lee of Bridgeman Road, who displayed herself for the titillation of the Bridgeman Gang. This service was performed behind a truck on the railway sidings, for which she charged one penny – but no touching. I was far too young to be a member of the gang, but she always took my penny!

Then there were my teachers at the council school. I see them so clearly, their faces, their clothes, even their mannerisms. Mr Ellis, for example, over six foot tall, thin as a rake with spidery legs, an early John Cleese doing his 'funny walk'. He had the habit of rubbing the clenched fist of his right hand against the open palm of his left. This was confusing inasmuch as it meant he was either pleased or very angry – and we never knew which until it was too late! So it was best to sit very still and upright at one's desk – and pray.

Mr Jones, maths, wore a black jacket and waistcoat with striped trousers and a pince-nez either hanging around his neck or perched precariously on his nose. Thus dressed he played football with us at lunchtime where his behaviour can only be likened to Brian Glover's as the schoolteacher in Ken Loach's wonderful film, *Kes*. Mr Jones totally monopolized the game, taking sole charge of the ball and not letting anyone else get a look in. Try as we might to tackle him, we bounced off this manic figure like so many rubber ducks. Occasionally one of us out of sheer frustration would endanger, if not life, certainly limb by falling on the ball, making it impossible for Mr Jones to retrieve it. He would then claim a foul and promptly award a free kick – to himself.

There is one other I must mention – Miss Wilson. She taught history and art and was a goddess of loveliness, wafting a beautiful aroma in the midst of the horde of unwashed schoolboys. She occasionally sat on the corner of her table, one leg extended to the floor, revealing an expanse of thigh which always induced us to drop our pencils and whilst retrieving them take a look up her skirts, a most popular diversion!

At an early age, according to my mother, I was already beginning to show a willingness to entertain – 'showing off' as she called it. Hitherto, any talent for entertaining in our family manifested itself only in my father's rendition of 'Burlington Bertie' and my mother's tearjerking, full-blooded version of 'The Sunshine of Your Smile'. There was, of course, the rumour of my grandfather bringing the house down playing the spoons. My granny also spoke of her embarrassment when she took me to the Weslyan Chapel 'Old Folks Home' where I gatecrashed the stage and recited a little poem she had taught me.

> On Monday we had bread and dripping
> On Tuesday we had dripping and bread
> On Wednesday and Thursday by way of a change
> We just had the dripping instead.

I've heard it said that an only child is a lonely child. This surely must depend on the child's circumstances. I spent most of my waking hours either at school or playing with my mates on the street, come rain or shine, and only after that final threat from my mother – 'You wait till your father gets home!' would I reluctantly go indoors. Once indoors, however, where there was no communication with anyone my age, I was prompted to create my own imaginary characters and, in the secrecy of the little bedroom I shared with my grandmother, act out my own fantasies.

So my life had begun and, with the die cast, the assumption, as with all working-class families at that time, was that an ordained pattern would follow. School until I was fourteen, leave and get a job – any job, choice of employment was rare indeed – find a girl, living no further perhaps than a few streets away, get married, live near our parents who soon would become grandparents, and thus the accepted cycle would continue. This was, after all, the recognized concept of what life was all about. To expect much more was to court disappointment – and deserved at that.

It was 1926, the General Strike, and Acton High Street and its surrounding thoroughfares were alive with uniforms – soldiers, police and special constables were everywhere to be seen, 'plus-four Johnnies', the civilian volunteers, were driving buses, protected by armed guards, and motorized military rode here and there chasing red banners. The revolutionaries had already taken over the Town Hall, the day of reckoning was at hand and my father, now a communist, was in the thick of it.

As far back as I can remember we had always been a Labour household, as were all the others at our end of Bridgeman

Road. To boast of a Tory vote by advertising the local candidate in your front window was just asking for a brick!

But this was violence, as our schoolmaster had warned us, 'Such people who would threaten the British way of life must be put down!' On my way home from school one day I saw my father struck to the ground by police when he tried to pull a 'plus-four' from the seat of his bus.

Sitting down with us that night, the first time for days, my mother tended his head wound as he regaled us with the story of how he and others had stormed a small, local engineering works. It seems the workers had ignored the order to stop work, so my father and his comrades stood over the machines, carrying pick-axes, threatening to smash them if the switches weren't pulled – they were. He went on, eyes alight, speaking to me of the end of capitalism, equal opportunities for us all ... the workers shall inherit the earth ... arise ye starving from your slumbers!

So I listened, somewhat confused. Was it really as simple as that, the haves and the have-nots? But, far more important, was this man sitting before me with bandaged head and bloodied shirt, so full of anger and revenge, was this my father? Was this the same man I had seen as a wee boy on holiday, with all those soldiers standing to attention, so proud in his uniform as 'God Save the King' was played and who bowed a servile head out of respect for his superiors?

Was this the man who had returned to, and suffered from, a country unfit for a hero to live in, where dole queues, insults and humiliation arising from seeking work that didn't exist, were the norm, and which I thought he was enduring with forbearance? A rhetorical question if ever there was one, for he was an amalgam of all those things, the father, soon to become the friend, whom I grew to admire and love.

There was no revolution. My mother continued to iron rich men's shirts from eight in the morning until six at night, Monday to Friday. My father returned to his place in the dole queue and my grandmother continued to deliver unwanted mites into an unwelcoming world. But whilst my father preached to me of a socialist utopia, and even bought me a copy of Robert Tressell's novel *The Ragged Trousered Philanthropists* for my fourteenth birthday, I gave socialism only my divided attention, having other interests at the time.

Charlie Burton is my one life-long friend, born at number 12 Bridgeman Road, six months my junior and brought into the world, of course, by my granny. Our mothers were quite friendly, whilst our friendship, to judge from ancient photographs taken at the weddings of both his aunt and his uncle in which we both appear, began in the cradle. But if memory serves me correctly it was around the age of ten or so that our relationship really began to develop due to the fact that Charlie by this time could play the piano well, and I had a singing voice that could already do things with a song. This had come to light when we won a talent competition at our local cinema – first prize five shillings between us! Dubbing our act 'The It Kids – A Song in Harmony', we launched ourselves on to an eagerly awaiting public – at the poorer end of Bridgeman Road, that is. And, no doubt due to our youth and cheek, we became a very popular little act around West London working-men's clubs, which lasted until our teens when we moved on to dance bands. Then came a girlfriend and love, for Charlie and Elsie, but not for me, although Elsie swears I was the first to court her. They eventually got married, but wedlock wasn't for me, my appetite for entertaining had been well and truly whetted.

I was not, however, aware of any particular interest in theatre or acting until I was eighteen, being quite content to sing for my supper. Then came a matter of unrequited love to upset the apple cart. The young lady, whose name I cannot now recall, was a very keen actress and a member of the Acton Co-operative Players, and she could well have been the reason for my decision to have a go at 'this acting lark'.

With any experience, of course, it would have been immediately apparent to me that this was no average bunch of amateurs. Being part of the Workers Educational Association programme sponsored by the Co-operative Society, with a repertory that included such playwrights as Galsworthy, Kaiser and Shaw, it was clear that the social implications of the plays were of more importance than any self-indulgence on the part of the actors.

The choice of play and players, direction and any tutorials were the sole responsibility of Meg Thomas, a delightful middle-aged lady who helped me discover a natural instinct for acting and proceeded to demand more. It was as if I became her challenge, instinct wasn't enough; I must understand the reason for what I was doing and why. So began my first lessons in the never-ending process of learning about acting. The only memory I have of the plays in which I appeared was an English translation of a German play by Georg Kaiser, a confederate of Bertholt Brecht, called *Gas*.

Inevitably our teacher–pupil relationship was a close one and, although she was old enough to be my mother, I developed an almost uncontrollable passion for her. It was a difficult situation for Meg and, as the intimacy between us grew, almost impossible to control. Finally, her resistance gave way. What followed was my first and probably the most gentle, wonderful sexual experience of my life. I recommend such an introduction to all adolescent male virgins.

My eighteenth birthday had come and gone, and I was getting nowhere fast. I had been pulled up in my tracks just as I had thought I was breaking away from that seemingly inevitable golden rule of getting a regular job. Years before, my old headmaster had told my mother, 'There is little point in me keeping William any longer.' And with that encouraging news she abandoned any illusion she may have had about seeing me off every morning, City-bound and clutching a briefcase filled with sandwiches. But if that wasn't to be, then I'd better find *something*. I found Alfie Taylor. We had met at a local engineering factory where I'd taken a night job and, lifting me out of the monotony of that place, he imbued me with something of his enthusiasm, optimism and belief in the future. He was in fact just the tonic I needed. Now he reminds me of Dickens's Mr Jingles, and he had a personality just as infectious. Together we threw in our jobs and set up a window-cleaning business. We had no money, but as Alfie said, 'Who needs capital? Anyone can clean a window!' Our gimmick was to pay for any panes broken. As I say, he was long on enthusiasm, but short on entrepreneurial acumen. I broke a window pane the first week and we were out of business.

'Never mind,' says Alfie. 'It's a terrible job in the winter!' After several board meetings at our local hostelry we decided to try our luck as door-to-door salesmen or 'on the knocker' as it was called then. How we did it I don't know but we scraped together sufficient cash to buy stock from a shady wholesale warehouse in Aldgate.

Poplin shirts at three shillings and sixpence, woollen pullovers at two shillings and sixpence, with a bargain line in socks at fourpence a pair! How could we go wrong? Easily! We were ignorant of the time-honoured principle of being on the knocker, which is 'here today and gone tomorrow'. Instead we sold our wares to friends and relatives – a fatal error. Within a few days the first repercussions were apparent. Our pullovers had never seen sheep, something very odd had happened to our so-called poplin shirts during the ironing and, most embarrassing of all, the socks dissolved when dropped into boiling water!

My mother took the brunt of the complaints and my father, unsportingly I thought, demanded his money back. The few friends we had approached sent us to Coventry and, with Alfie's big brother looming significantly, we felt a new element of risk had been added to our venture that had not been anticipated in the market research. We quickly flogged off the remaining stock, at a loss, naturally, and went into liquidation; quite literally – taking ourselves to the Vale Tavern where we proceeded to get ever so slightly Brahms and totally Liszt.

*

With my twenty-first birthday come and gone, my mother seemed happier for me. She spoke to friends of my 'settling down', which, to her, meant that the logic of my life had begun to prevail. After all, I had held down a job for over a year, working at Eastmans & Sons, a large firm of dyers and cleaners where I was trained to remove spots from men's clothing. It was tedious but undemanding. I was also courting, seriously. A non-thespian, her name was Jennie Watts and she lived nearby. The preordained pattern was falling into place.

At this time the only relief to the monotony was my activity with Eastmans Dramatic Society, organized by Miss Violet Heald, the Welfare Officer and a keen amateur thespian. I can't say that the repertoire of plays which included *The Bishop's Candlesticks* and *The Eye of the Beholder* had the excitement or adventure of the Co-op Players, but at least it was 'make believe' and there wasn't much of that around any more.

It was after the first night of one of our shows when we had all gathered for a drink that Violet took me aside and said, almost accusingly, 'What are you doing wasting your life in a factory?' I countered, as I thought, logically, by asking what she thought I should be doing, options being short in W4. She said that I was 'born to act' and that that was what I 'should be doing'. She went on to say all the things I'd ever wanted to hear.

'If you don't act, it will be a terrible waste and I'll never forgive you!' she concluded. Then she kissed me. I thought of Meg Thomas, but Jennie appeared and was ready to go home. As we walked Jennie said, 'Miss Heald likes you, doesn't she?' Putting my arm around her, I replied, 'She's old enough to be my mother.'

Saying goodnight on her doorstep we got around to the inevitable subject of betrothal. I usually listened in silence, but that night, no doubt fired by Violet's words, I cut the subject short with 'I'm going to be an actor, you know.' Fully prepared for some kind of remonstration, bitterness or even jealousy, I was taken aback when she enquired seriously, 'How can someone like you be an actor?' She was right, of course. That was the question, not to be, but *how* to be? How did a working-class man like me become an actor? What did I have to do? Where did I have to go? Certainly not to the Labour Exchange. I obviously had to get acquainted with someone who knew the answer to all the whys and wherefores. But who? We never went to the theatre or a concert. For live entertainment we went to the local variety theatre.

When I got home my mother was waiting up. Dad, now a trolley-bus driver, was on late shift. As she made the tea she enquired how the play had gone. I told her very well and that we'd had a good audience. She looked at me thoughtfully. 'You know, Billy,' she said, 'I reckon if you keep up this acting, Miss Heald would see you have a job for life.' I drank my tea.

2

The End of the Beginning

My memories of my life since the day I decided I was going to be an actor are inextricably bound up with my acting career. Every important event in my non-acting life I remember in relation to some point in my acting life, or reminds me of what the thespian me was doing. Thus, if reminded of the death of my father, I immediately recall being led around the parade ring at Newmarket, astride a horse called Bountiful, during the making of *The Rainbow Jacket*, and a young assistant giving me a message saying I was to phone my wife as soon as possible. The news of my mother's passing came in the early hours of the morning of my opening night as Ko-Ko in *The Mikado* at Sadlers Wells. It was during a performance at the Players Theatre that I was informed of the birth of my son and, having duly celebrated, found that I was only kept on my feet for the curtain call with the aid of Hattie Jaques's strong right arm! I am sure I'm not alone in relating life to work.

The opportunity for me to break with the preordained pattern came as a bolt from the blue, when I received a letter from a Captain Frank Bond, manager of Warners Holiday Camp in Dovercourt. He was offering me a job as entertainer for the season commencing Easter 1937. This apparently was in consequence of a holiday I'd spent with some workmates the

16

previous year at Warners camp in Devon. It seems I had been the life and soul of the party, much to the delight of the other campers and Captain Bond had taken due note. There was no hesitation, no ifs or buts. I immediately gave notice to Eastman & Sons, and Jennie Watts did likewise to me. Breaking off our engagement was probably the most sensible thing that dear girl ever did in her life. I was totally selfish. I was being offered a chance that might never come again and, win or lose, I grabbed it. I worked fourteen hours a day, six days a week for which I was paid thirty-five shillings and my keep – I was a pro!

My job as entertainer certainly had its perks. That is, if one had the necessary initiative and hustle. For example, on Monday mornings it was my task to lead a hike, always announced over the loudspeakers thus: 'Now, don't forget Bill is leading a hike before lunch; discover with him the delights of our local scenery. All those wishing to join him should meet by the swimming pool at eleven o'clock.' So off we'd all go, no doubt singing 'We're happy when we're hiking'. And there I was at the head of a band of merry footsloggers numbering sixty or seventy eager souls.

The idea was to set a good pace, up and down a few lanes, and across a couple of fields, just enough to give the impression that we had covered a few miles and wouldn't the sight of a pub be most welcome? Then, lo and miraculously behold, there it was! I'd say, 'Well, I don't know about you lot but I could do with a pint.' They followed me to a man and woman. Coincidentally Mine Host would be ready and waiting with his staff and entire family, hands poised over pumps. In a very short time everyone was outside again lazing in the sun with their drinks. Here we would stay, despite the feeble protestations of the few teetotallers, until it was time to return for lunch. This never took long as we were never more than 800 yards from the camp.

Later I would return to the pub for a quiet drink before the evening's festivities began. Before I left I would have been, shall we say, rewarded for the custom I had inadvertently brought in. But there was one time when I thought the landlord had short-changed me, a touch mean with the 'dropsy'. The following Monday I phoned him suggesting that he wait outside the pub to welcome us. Sure enough, there he was, smiling until I led my thirsty followers past him and on to another pub down the road. Don't mention the Godfather to me. I could have made Marlon Brando look like Peter Pan!

I sent a little home each week but my mother, in order to make ends meet, took in a lodger. Phillip McConnell was a builder's labourer by trade and, coincidentally, a keen amateur actor. Naturally this gave us an immediate affinity when we met at the end of my season. He was involved at that time with the popular left-wing Unity Theatre, housed in a converted chapel in a back street of Somers Town, King's Cross. It was an amateur theatre insofar as the actors weren't paid and, because of its politics it was a club theatre, which meant that it was necessary to become a member in order to see a performance. The sole reason for this was to avoid the dictatorial powers of the Lord Chamberlain who exercised the right to say what could or could not be played or said. Whilst almost entirely maintained by the trades unions, it nevertheless had some eminent names amongst its membership, luminaries such as H G Wells, George Bernard Shaw, Sean O'Casey, Dame Sybil Thorndike, Flora Robson, Tyrone Guthrie, and Victor Gollancz, to mention but a few. And Unity could boast the fact that it was the first theatre in this country to introduce the plays of the sixteenth-century Spanish playwright, Lope de Vega with its production of *Fuente Ovejuna* in 1938. Also, with such a large and willing company of actors, which down the years spawned such names as Maxine Audley, Bob Hoskins, Michael Gambon, David Kossoff, John Slater, Vida Hope, Alfie Bass – and myself – it was possible to maintain a permanent repertory of plays, musicals and revues which, because of their social content, would not only attract new writers in this country but also from abroad, such as Bertholt

Brecht, Clifford Odets and Irwin Shaw. It was not only writers who came to Unity from abroad. Phillip's involvement at that time was in a new American play, *Plant in the Sun* written by Ben Bengal, the leading role of which was played by Paul Robeson who had come over specifically to do so, paying all his own expenses.

I was asked recently on a breakfast TV show what I thought might have happened to me if *Last of the Summer Wine* hadn't come about. I pointed out that what would perhaps have been a far more interesting question, was what would have happened to me if my mother had not decided to take a lodger who just happened to be interested in the Unity Theatre and who persuaded me to give an audition in October 1938 for the satirical pantomime *Babes in the Wood*, in which I got a part when it opened in November of that year.

Then, on 11 July 1939, while I was working at Dovercourt Holiday Camp, I received a letter which began:

Dear Bill,
This is to advise you that your name was put forward to be included in the short list of Unity actors for the Kingsway Theatre, which will be on a professional basis. At the Management meeting last Thursday, your name was accepted.

The play chosen to mark Unity's début at the Kingsway Theatre was one by Ernst Toller, *Pastor Neimuller*, to be directed by Lewis Casson, but which the Lord Chamberlain suddenly saw fit to ban because he considered it to be too anti-Nazi: this only within a month or so of the outbreak of war. But Unity, forever used to such crises, immediately transferred the play scheduled for the little theatre at King's Cross to become the opening production at the Kingsway. This was a new play, *Colony*, by Geoffrey Trease, dealing with unionism among the plantation workers in the West

Indies, and we began rehearsals under the direction of Herbert Marshall.

It was during the second week of rehearsal that Herbert suddenly called us together after an urgent phone call. He said, 'I have to inform you that the Management Committee have decided to abandon the Kingsway Theatre project because information has been received that war is being declared on Sunday.' I can still hear the silence that followed. The whole company was stunned by the news. And although not a word had been mentioned, I'm sure we all had secretly lived with the fear of what was now inevitable.

I've had my share of disappointments in life, but never one to equal that. There were no fond farewells, no cries of 'Good luck' or 'See you around'. It seemed we just silently collected our belongings and crept away. I remember standing outside the Kingsway Theatre feeling utterly lost, not knowing what to do or where to go. The bottom had fallen out of my world.

It was a bright, sunny day, traffic rushed to and fro, laughing office girls, out for a lunchtime stroll, were ogled by young bucks, lovers clung shamelessly to one another and people hurried by to pointless business meetings. Didn't they know? Didn't they care? Or were they just living in the hope of a miracle between now and Sunday, one that would save us from the anticipated carnage? Then why couldn't we actors have been left in limbo to carry on with our make-believe?

Very depressed, I phoned Marcel, a girlfriend who loved me more than I deserved. She left her office straight away and took me to lunch, then back to her flat and bed. It was during a lull over a cup of tea that she asked if she might stay with me over the coming weekend. She had no family and didn't particularly want to be alone at such a time.

Although I was more than willing, home to me now was a little terraced, two-small-down, three-even-smaller-up rooms, no bathroom, a washhouse the size of a telephone kiosk, with gas stove and sink (where cooking and ablutions had to take place – occasionally at the same time) plus an outside loo. My

mother called it cosy, and who were Dad and I to argue? We
were used to it. But we'd never had anyone to stay! Still, it
was a time for families to be together. Phillip had gone back
to Ireland and I had promised Mum I'd be home.

So I took Marcel with me, deciding to let her discover the
domestic disarrangements for herself.

Came the war that fatal Sunday morning, and we gathered
around the wireless to await Mr Chamberlain's official
announcement that hostilities had begun with Germany, which
struck me as an ominous formality. Some had already predicted
the outcome of his abortive visit to Berchtesgaden and the
pathetic naivety of the Peace in our Time message, but we'd
been cheering too loudly to pay attention. So there we were,
my mother, Marcel and I, still in our night attire and dressing
gowns, drinking endless cups of tea as we waited. My father,
quite unconcerned, tended his postage-stamp garden, continuing to do so in spite of the wailing of the air-raid siren
that followed the declaration of war. But for us it meant an
immediate assumption that Hitler had already arrived and was
at that very moment pin-pointing the Rowbothams' residence
for a direct hit!

Panicking, I took command and ordered the ladies to seek
cover under the hedge at the bottom of the garden which
divided us from the allotments. This necessitated our squeezing
through a narrow gap. I think I should explain that my mother
was not built for squeezing through anything! For folk like us
in those days, if you were fat, you were fat, and that was that.
Unfortunately she fell into a frame of runner beans and Marcel
fell on top of her. Eventually, however, we were concealed
under the hedge – at least I thought so. I mean, who in Hell's
name expects to find people watching over their parsnips in
the midst of an air raid! But they were. Husband and wife and
an air-raid warden staring at us agape. Some twit sitting under
a hedge with a pretty girl in a torn négligé and an elderly lady
wearing a string of runner beans!

*

One of the great things about being a part of Unity Theatre was the resilience, it rubbed off on you; the confidence, too, in what you were doing, the ability to deal with any situation that might arise. But I must admit to taking stock after the collapse of the Kingsway Theatre project. The sudden disappearance of the General Secretary, the later discovery that the bank balance from *Babes in the Wood* was far short of the official receipts, and finally a Government ban on all live entertainment was surely sufficient to put a halt to any activity for a while? But no, a press notice was issued, informing all and sundry that Unity Theatre would open with a new revue, *Sandbag Follies*, as soon as the ban on live entertainment was lifted. We had the title, all we needed was the show!

True to the word, with the lifting of the ban after a matter of weeks, a meeting was called for the following weekend summoning all the creative talent we could muster, with the object of writing a revue which could open the following Tuesday!

I won't attempt to list the famous names that dropped in over that weekend to offer their services. I had two roles as compère and producer and, without anyone's permission, threw in my variety act which was devoid of any social significance, but went very well.

I think I ought to mention at this point that despite my background and the teachings of my father, which must have had something to do with my immediate response to Unity Theatre, I still had very little, if any, political convictions at the time. I had been successful at Dovercourt and was promoted to Entertainments Manager with a staff of one and an increase in salary of fifteen shillings. But during the winter my little world was taken up with scraping a living elsewhere. This consisted of the dole and a few band gigs with which I could just about get by. So, *Sandbag Follies* for me, whilst I enjoyed working my butt off, was just a showcase.

We opened on schedule – just – the first theatre to do so

throughout the land, despite the Windmill Theatre's boast, 'We Never Closed'. The production costs were six shillings and ninepence – the price of a tin of blackout paint. To observe on the opening night that it had been under-rehearsed would have been a compliment! For example, I received the lyrics of the song meant to open the second half of the show just as I was walking on to open the second half. So the audience and I learned it together. However, with some changes it was honed into a great little show and audiences came in their droves and loved it!

What is probably my most vivid memory of Dovercourt Holiday Camp had very little to do with holidays. There was a war on, the camp closed and everyone had run home to the blackout, which was exactly how I discovered it a couple of months later in the darkness of a winter's afternoon. I was there in response to a phone call that morning from Frank Bond asking me to come down immediately. There was, he had said, an emergency the details of which he couldn't discuss on the phone. He sounded more like *James* Bond! It was impossible to believe that only weeks ago the place had rung with the joyful laughter of children and families, and the sighs of eternal love that would fade with the end of the holiday. There was barbed wire everywhere, the swimming pool was now an ammunition dump and a concrete gun emplacement replaced the ice-cream and candyfloss kiosk.

In the warmth of his office, Frank explained that the camp had been taken over as a temporary reception area for some Jewish refugee children from the Continent who were being smuggled out of France under cover of darkness that very night. My first reaction to this dramatic situation was What did he want from me? He explained that apart from assisting him with the day-to-day routine, I also might 'Help cheer them up a bit.' I think his actual phrase was 'Give 'em a laugh.' Did any of them speak English? He doubted it. Thanks, Frank!

And so we waited, the doctors, the Jewish welfare admin-istrators, cooks, nurses, the domestic staff, all of us, I'm certain, unsure and apprehensive – after all, there was no guarantee that the boat would arrive. The waiting seemed endless, but finally the news came that the boat had docked and the girls would be with us very soon. There was a great cheer of relief, and some tears. The dance hall had been converted into a reception area with the overhead strip lighting reduced to the minimum. This gave the girls' initial entrance an almost ghost-like effect. In single file they followed one another, each carrying a small bundle or battered suitcase, their only possessions. How many there were I can't recall, but all so solemn, which was hardly surprising. The older girls were only too aware they would probably never see their parents again. I held out my arms in welcome, but they drew away in fear as they were led to the dining room for supper, a meal I shall always remember as the most silent and saddest of my life.

I hung around for a few days, lending a hand where I could. With the help of some local musical talent, several evenings of entertainment were arranged, and, with due modesty, I have to confess to being the hit of the show. I'd found the real answer to the language barrier. As old-fashioned and boring as it would no doubt seem today in this age of pre-packaged humour, I concluded my professional variety act with a short series of mime, a humorous mirror to everyday occurrences: a drunk trying to find the keyhole to open his front door, an over-confident goalkeeper, and many more. This proved to be an ideal means of communication and really did 'give 'em a laugh'. In fact they were almost hysterical over my impression of a lady undressing to take a bath. Forty-five years later came an epilogue to this strange story when I received a letter from an elderly lady who, as a young girl, had been one of those who had landed that night on these dark and foreign shores which had since become home. She told me that some of them had kept in touch and were now planning a grand reunion at which they would like me to be their guest of honour. Sadly, I had to decline this invitation as I was on location – in Yorkshire, of course.

The thought of war has always been abhorrent to me and when in 1940 the call came to join the colours and heed the demand that my country needed me, I fell back, as always, on my father's advice, succinct and very much to the point: 'Observe the rules and don't volunteer for anything.' He also took the trouble to secrete in my small cardboard suitcase a packet of Condy's Crystals (a few dissolved in warm water will harden the soles of the feet) and a packet of French letters. The accompanying note said tersely, 'Never be without 'em.'

I found myself in the Royal Pioneer Corps. I gave my civilian occupation as actor-entertainer, and within a week or so of settling down to army life under canvas in the Welsh hills I was duly sent for by the Regimental Sergeant-Major. He was a tall, physically overpowering man who frightened the daylights out of me when I presented myself to him. But off the barrack square I discovered he spoke with a soft Celtic brogue which went a long way to charming me into accepting the responsibility for forming a concert party. He was a bit showbiz crazy and played the mouth organ, reminding me of this several times during our first meeting. Of course he was 'in', wasn't he? I mean, Regimental Sergeant-Major! I also thought it opportune to tell him that time would be needed for writing scripts, attending rehearsals etc., and in consequence, I was relieved of all duties other than basic training!

My first leave took me back to Unity, where I hoped everything would be as usual, but I was in for a rude awakening. The bombing of London was at its height and performances of Robert Mitchell's play *The Matchgirls*, the story of the Bryant and May's strike of 1888, had been reduced to two matinees at weekends. The roof was devoid of slates due to a near-miss by a land-mine and, of course, it rained – the only time I've sat in a theatre under an umbrella! There were very few people to be seen, just a sparse audience, a couple of technicians and the cast.

There were many stories of their heroic dedication to keep the play running. They literally risked life and limb with every performance. Girls were injured, and two kiiled travelling to and from the theatre whilst braving the air raids. It all seemed so weird, unreal, the noise of rain on my umbrella, a dog barking in a nearby garden and the winter night sky above. On stage I watched, in spite of the odds, of even death itself, the seemingly defiant performances – the show must go on! And when the curtain fell it seemed to me the drama went on, as those present showed their appreciation then hurried away into the accentuated darkness of the black-out with the hope of being home before the siren wailed. I spent every night of that leave in an Anderson shelter with my mother, but the ghosts of that afternoon were to walk with me for some time to come.

Back in barracks, I followed my father's advice and accepted the discipline and ritual, the mindless bullshit and the fact that it was necessary for the Sergeant to yell his instructions at me from a distance of a couple of inches. In fact I buckled down so well I was offered a commission. And who, I ask you, was the officer commanding the Officer Cadet Training Unit? None other than Colonel Frank Bond, my holiday camp boss! I passed out with flying colours.

Later, with the assistance of my NCOs, I was in charge of putting the Brigadier's Headquarters staff through their battle training. It was during one of the classes that my corporal, unknowingly, entered the danger area of an unexploded hand grenade. Tragically he had a foot blown off. This is a memory I have never erased from my mind. My immediate reaction was to hide and I remember locking myself in a hut. I have further, vague memories of being hospitalized and the determined efforts of the staff to prevent me causing further damage to my right shin which I was unconsciously rubbing down to the bone. Significantly it was the right leg from which the corporal had lost his foot. Psychiatry couldn't help and I was left to a self-imposed silence and resignation.

After my discharge my mother held me close and with tears in her eyes offered that good old panacea that Londoners know so well, 'I'll make a nice cup of tea.' My father whilst seemingly sympathetic and understanding, showed little emotion. In fact I felt his disappointment. But it was he who eventually interrupted my voluntarily imposed isolation by pointing out that despite the war, life still had to go on, and wasn't it about time I realized it?

So I went back to Unity Theatre where I was welcomed as if I'd never been away. It was only a few weeks later when my friend Alfie Bass told me he had got his calling-up papers and suggested my name to take over the role of Gunner Cohen in the James Bridie play *Mr Bolfry*, starring Alistair Sim, at the Playhouse Theatre. I was apprehensive, but it was a challenge, it seemed a lifetime since I had even thought of acting. Life had suddenly become real. Could I do it any more? But Alfie wasn't taking no for an answer, he had already fixed an audition for me.

So the war that had been responsible for thwarting my first opportunity as a professional actor was to be the reason for my second – also in London's West End. But not for long. A second blitz had begun and so it was with relief that we learned the play was going on tour. Now I was to have my first experience of theatrical landladies and their various concepts of comfort and cleanliness in wild and strange places like Glasgow and Bridlington. During the war the only means of transport for theatre companies was by train and as we always travelled on Sundays the service could be almost as unreliable and precarious as it is today – without hostilities! Yet there was a foolproof system in those days to ensure that all the actors, technicians, scenery and props, etc. arrived at the next place of performance all at the same time and on the same day. It was very simple. A carriage was booked for the entire company and a truck for the impedimenta would be hitched to the back of the train and off we'd all jolly well go. Now, invariably you had to change at Doncaster, it was a kind of ritual this gathering of show-business folk on a Sunday morning, the platform alive with thespians and variety acts, conversing across railway lines in their own particular lingo, an example of which was given to me by Leslie Henson.

'*Thespians*'

Aged Actor 1 If it's such a small part, Teddy, is it worthwhile playing?

Aged Actor 2 Oh yes, there's a sumptuous dinner scene in the second act!

'*Variety*'

Comic 1 Ow'd yer do last week then, Charlie?

Comic 2 Washers!
(Poor take at the box office!)

Comic 1 What about yer billing?

Comic 2 Wines and spirits.
(Small type, bottom of the bill.)

There is a type of theatrical landlady who posts her rules on a notice-board in the hallway. She abides by them rigorously and, by heck, if you want a quiet week you'll do the same! Before you've had a chance to put your suitcase down it's 'Breakfast is from 8.30 to 9.30, please give notice before taking a bath and no music after midnight!'

Then there is another type, best described as the Mrs Rottweilers, the con ladies. These keep a permanently dirty rim round the bath, knowing full well no one will dare take a bath in it; they measure single meagre rations of breakfast cornflakes into empty Kelloggs packets, kept especially for the purpose.

Of course, I speak of a bygone age, of war, its aftermath, suffering and shortages, when we ate food that today we would hesitate to put before the family pet. We also shared the blackout, that dark shadow which fell, enveloping reality, becoming a black void. The only indications of life were the hurrying footsteps of never-to-be-seen strangers, the whine of passing trolley buses, the sudden barking of a dog, maybe a peal of laughter, sounds immediately lost in the dark.

Thus it was that I arrived at Newcastle near five o'clock one Sunday afternoon, for the first time in my life. I groped my way to the taxi rank. Of course there were no taxis – after all, it was late afternoon. As I stood there staring into the blackness, the thought struck me that I would probably have to remain rooted to the spot until early-morning light because I hadn't the faintest idea where I was. There was simply nothing to see and if the deafening silence that surrounded me was any indication, there was absolutely no one abroad in Newcastle, just me. What a relief, then, when a taxi finally came into blurred view, and a cheerful driver too. That was until I gave him the address. 'You'll be at the theatre, then,' he remarked, almost with a note of sympathy. Kindly, he helped me with my bags to the front door. 'Best of luck,' he called out, the note of sympathy now one of commiseration. The taxi disappeared into the nothingness.

It was my fourth knock, which almost took the door off its hinges, that eventually brought some sign of life. Amid much scuffling and shouting accompanied by a barking dog – a voice called from somewhere, 'Shut up, yer daft bugger!' – the door was finally opened and there she stood, a vision of a disordered, ravaged Nora Batty. The hallway smelt of stale cabbage and as I followed her up the stairs I had the sinking feeling that I had touched bottom. This was confirmed when she threw open a door announcing, 'This is me guest room.' Lino on the floor, a single gas mantle flickering, one bucket of coal which, I was informed, was to last the week and seemed to me to be more than adequate when I saw the size of the fireplace. In one corner, under a minute window, was a grey and gaunt bed, and in the centre of the room a large ginger cat was asleep on the 'dining' table. 'Shoo, Polly,' screamed Mrs Rottweiler, as she cleared the cat from the table and out on to the landing in one swoop. 'I've got something hot for your tea,' she said, moving to the door. She managed to make it sound menacing. Suddenly, I had lost my appetite. 'Oh, by the way, I won't have any hanky-panky here.' With that she was gone.

What an exit line. Hanky-panky? Young buck as I was then, even I found it impossible to relate sexual pleasure to such macabre surroundings.

The 'something hot' for my tea turned out to be a boiled lukewarm haddock, a little margarine, a large loaf and a pot of tea. It was then I had my second doubt about this acting lark.

'Not much of a night for going out,' she called, catching me at the front door. 'Just a walk before bed,' I replied, clutching firmly behind my back the paper bag which contained the offending fish, to be dumped as I set out to find somewhere to eat.

When I returned she had cleared the table, except for the loaf of bread and it was the last thing I saw as I wearily closed my eyes. Thus it was the first thing I saw when I awoke. Well, it was more Polly than loaf as she drooped over it in slumber. I didn't touch that loaf all week and Mrs Rottweiler never took it into her head to remove it. Polly was very pleased.

However, all was forgotten the following week when we played Aberdeen and, at some theatre function or other, I was introduced to Edith Harris who had escaped from Glasgow with her young daughter Zan, following a disastrous marriage and, as she described it, 'the suffocation of a loving family'. Was it a mutual, instant, affinity? Was it the immediate empathy of two lonely souls? Or was it 'love at first sight'? The latter, for Edith, in her present circumstances, represented a cliché of which she was, understandably, wary. As for me, almost thirty, I had never before experienced such empathy. As the tour of the play ended in Aberdeen I stayed on until my money ran out, by which time Edith and I were pretty confident that the die had been cast.

Forced by lack of money, I returned to London and a full-time job at Unity Theatre as Outside Show Organizer which I very soon built up into a much needed travelling entertainment company. There were four small mobile groups of amateur entertainers who travelled to factory canteens, air raid shelters and anywhere workers were getting on with the task of trying to win the war.

Looking back through a fog of memories, adventures, and misadventures of those early outside shows, I recall entertaining the night shift at The Royal Mint which was all a bit 'make do and mend', having been evacuated somewhere else in the City. We performed in the canteen to a very appreciative audience. Then having been given supper, we were informed it was impossible to leave because there was an air raid taking place. So they found us a quiet corner and some bunk beds. That should have been one for the *Guinness Book of Records*, three strangers asleep in The Royal Mint, amidst all that money!

On another occasion, we had just finished a show on an underground platform for those taking shelter there – 'we' being Doris Levinson, a fine jazz singer, Benny Norris on accordion and myself – when, as we waited for a train to take us on to the next station and a repeat performance, a bomb was dropped, destroying part of the station entrance above. The immediate reaction on the platform was one of panic. But Doris stepped back up on to the little rostrum and began to sing 'Some of These Days'. She didn't sing it to them, she sang it *at* them, almost ablaze with anger. She was glorious!

> 'You're gonna miss my hugging
> You're gonna miss my kissing
> You're gonna miss me, honey
> When I'm far away!'

She was willing them not to panic, but to stand and sing with

her – and they did. Eventually the platform rang with their
voices. When she finally stepped down they cheered her, then
I took her into my arms and kissed her and they cheered again.
I loved Doris Levinson, but she loved Dave Abrahams. Ah,
well, that's the way the cookie crumbles!

As I have been telling this story I am reminded of a duet I
sang with Doris entitled 'One Big Union for Two' which came
from the show *Pins and Needles*. It was staged originally by
the International Ladies Garment Workers Union as an
amateur show performed by some of its members at weekends.
The original opening was on 27 November 1937 in New York
and from its humble beginnings was to become a Broadway
hit that ran for four years. It was the songs that interested me,
both lyrics and music written by Harold Rome, with titles
such as 'Doing the Reactionary', 'Sing me a Song of Social
Significance', 'It's Not Cricket to Picket' and 'It's Better with
a Union Man'. I have to admit they do not have the ring of a
Lloyd Webber musical, but Stanley Green, in his book *The
World of Musical Comedy*, writes of Rome, 'The ability to
express in songs the honest emotions of those who are least
articulate has been one of his most distinguishing charac-
teristics. For Rome is essentially a people's composer and
lyricist, one who without being sentimental or patronizing,
provides the common man with uncommon musical
expressions.'

Of which I consider the following lyric a supreme example.

VERSE

He I've decided the only way I can woo you
    Is to take a tip from the AF of L and the CIO.
She Now you're talking, perhaps I might listen to you.
    I won't say that I'll say yes and I won't say I'll say no.
He Then it's not too late to negotiate.
She Ah, well, we'll see, perhaps we can agree.
                    *

CHORUS

He I'm on a campaign to make you mine,
   I'll picket you until you sign
   In one big union for two
   No Courts injunction can make me stop
   Until your love is all closed shop
   In one big union for two
She Seven days a week you'll claim the right
   To make me yours both day and night–
   The hours may be long
He But fifty million union members can't be wrong.
Both When we have joined up perhaps there'll be
   A new recruit, or two or three,
   For that's what team work can do
   In one big union for two.

A similar pattern of such entertainment was introduced to Unity with the political pantomime, *Babes in the Wood* in 1938. It was in this that I sang the love duet, 'Love on the Dole', which was certainly never going to make the charts, despite the fact that Decca was bold enough to record it. In fact, the last time I heard the record was down the Portobello Road market being played on an old wind-up gramophone, balanced on a rickety old perambulator, pushed by an even older tramp. I offered to buy it for a half-crown; he told me to 'piss off'. Such is the price of fame!

The Way to the Stars (1945) is a classic war film of its time and, judging by its continual showing on TV, probably one of the most popular. It was certainly a film in which I was glad to be involved, the main reason being that it was my first role of any note in a feature film. This was no 'telling cameo', as agents are wont to describe some insignificant, momentary appearance to their clients, and I didn't get killed before the end of the first reel. This, I have to admit, was due no doubt to the fact that I was playing sergeant air gunner to John

Mills's fighter pilot and as long as he remained alive, I stayed in the film!

It was whilst we were filming this on location at RAF Catterick, that I formed such fond memories as arguing the role of theatre in society with Trevor Howard as we rode bicycles, both very drunk; Stanley Holloway patiently teaching me to play poker; and dear 'Puffin' Asquith, who directed the film so beautifully, who always had time to make me feel at ease. With due regard to Terence Rattigan who wrote the screen play, I thought the name 'Nobby Clarke' (the character I played) lacked a certain imagination. However, I had learned through experience, playing so many of these service types, that the name and rank were synonymous with the lower orders, such as the lads I had grown up with: Lynch, Potts, Doyle ... and even Rowbotham was abbreviated to 'Rawarse'! Yet I suppose there is a case to be made for such class distinction. For example, Lance-Corporal Peregrine Worsthorne, how could anyone be committed to jankers with a name like that?

3

Shadows and a Rank James Cagney

Leafing through one of my scrapbooks, I came across a single sheet of notepaper on which is written, in my handwriting, 'Conversation with soldier sweeping auditorium of Camp Theatre prior to play with Beatrix.' Beatrix Lehmann, a popular leading lady, was also a Patron of Unity Theatre and as such had asked me if I would partner her in the leading role in a play for the Forces. It was an honour and I must have accepted. I say 'must have' because I have no recollection of the play itself, nor its title, director, the other actors, rehearsals, nothing. And there is no further information on that piece of paper. It's extraordinary how the mind loves to play these tricks. However, what I do have are snatches of memory, vague shadows of recall rather like the faded photographs taken with a box Brownie. Three jigsaw-piece memories remain from that time, nevertheless. There's the Company train journey from Victoria Station when we were accompanied by an army officer carrying official War Office permits, allowing us to enter the town which was a 'no-go' area and which, for some reason, conjures up visions of empty streets. Then the few performances, travelling by coach through the blackest of black-outs, not knowing our destination and being none the wiser when we arrived. I did make an innocent enquiry of the Company manager as to our actual location, but all I got was a knowing wink and a 'Shh' which I duly passed on to anyone who asked me the same question. In fact the most vivid memory to emerge from these few shadows is of the entire Company, 'well stewed' after having been over-dined and over-wined in the Officer's Mess after the show, hysterically winking and shooshing at each other for the entire length of the return journey. Which brings me back to my note and the lone private soldier sweeping the theatre auditorium, it reads . . .

> ' 'Oo are you, then?'
> 'I'm doing a show here tonight, with Beatrix Lehmann.'
> 'Is she German?'
> 'I don't think so, perhaps her ancestors . . .'
> 'There's always some bleedin' excuse . . .' (pause) 'You a singer?'
> 'No, there's no singing.'
> 'Fank Christ fer that. Some of the NAAFI crap they serve us. Singers? My old man could fart better.'
> 'We're doing a play.'
> 'Play?'
> 'Yes . . . on stage.'
> (Long pause.)
> 'Oh, you mean actin' an' that.'
> 'Er . . . yes, acting and that. Will you be coming?'
> 'Me? No, I got my philosophy class tonight.'

But back to the affairs of the heart and that unfathomable thing called love which, with three hundred miles separating Edith and me, had developed into a spasmodic, stop-go sort of romance which was frustrating to say the least. In fact there was a danger of our devotion coming apart at the seams. So it needed very little effort on my part to persuade her to join me on a pre-London tour with a play called *Desert Rats*, written by Colin Morris. This decision I was to discover did not improve the on-going, strained relationship between Edith and her father, a self-made man who, beyond the stock market and owning race horses, saw his only other role as that of ruling his family. However, I will admit to a certain sympathy for the old man. Divorce wasn't such a popular sport in those days, it was a much more serious and certainly a much more prolonged procedure and in order to see his daughter get through with as little trouble and inconvenience as possible, he had hired the best lawyers in Glasgow. But what was his daughter doing during these delicate negotiations? She was chasing around the countryside with an actor! And a poor and unknown one to boot.

Desert Rats, as the title implies, was another war epic about a lost desert patrol, but with Richard Greene, the movie star, as the hero, we were assured of a success on the road. I played Trooper Bates, which was the smallest but best-written part in the play, as the critics were to point out. We opened at the Adelphi Theatre in London on 14 April 1945 to good reviews and a healthy reaction at the box office. But there was one unusual factor that seemed to overshadow this play about war – it was the prospect of peace. And the enemy was on the run.

I sat looking out of my dressing-room window at the joyous crowds parading up and down Maiden Lane, celebrating that first day of peace. No more inspirational speeches, no more flags, darkness or death. They just wanted to enjoy the relief of being able to get on with their lives once again. The notice to close *Desert Rats* followed almost at once.

Ted Willis, who was eventually to take his seat in the House of Lords had, like myself, begun his writing career at Unity Theatre. He went on to play an important role in both its management and repertory. During his time there he was able to practise his craft as a writer and with his play *Buster*, which was transferred to the Arts Theatre, began his successful career as a professional playwright. His beginnings were truly remarkable. For radio he wrote the first episode of *Mrs Dale's Diary*, for the theatre, *Woman in a Dressing Gown* (1962), for the cinema, *The Blue Lamp* and, with the coming of television, he created *Dixon of Dock Green*. It was Ted who during those early years at Unity suggested that I had served for long enough my apprenticeship as a writer of political and social satire, songs and musicals, etc. and the time had come for me to turn my attention to more serious drama. He proposed that I begin with an adaptation for the theatre of *The Ragged Trousered Philanthropists*. This was one novel I knew well, given to me, as I've said, by my father as a birthday present in my early teens and which, as far as memory will allow, was the extent of my serious reading at that time – with one exception, Henry James's *Turn of the Screw*. And although showing its age, I have it still, a handsome little volume with the inscription on its fly-leaf, 'This is the property of Bill Bolton and Bill Rowbotham, August, 1933.' It is before me as I write, but the reason for its acquisition remains a mystery. Bill Bolton was my cousin and we were classmates as children and friends throughout our teens and whilst I accept the fact that he was the better scholar, it has to be admitted that Henry James was not the most popular author among the working class of the mid-thirties. I have a vague memory of its purchase as being my idea, but why this classic tale?

There is also the discreet, pencilled price of six shillings, the equivalent of anything up to ten pounds at today's prices! My reading, I am pleased to say, has developed over the years and Mr James sits well among many others.

My cousin Bill died during the 1950s and with him the answer as to why we purchased that particular volume. For me, it has no attachment to faded memories and I ask the same questions each time I move house, rediscovering it as I unpack my books. Because I am sure my only serious reading at that time didn't extend beyond my mother's *Picture Show*, and although I am now well acquainted with the story as opera, play and film, the reason for my possession of that little volume must remain a mystery unsolved.

The Ragged Trousered Philanthropists tells the story of the restoration of a Victorian mansion to its former glory, during which we learn some of the dodges and skirting of corners by the contractors, Rushton and Co., in order to minimize costs. The reader is also drawn into the lives of the workers themselves; the plasterers, painters and paper-hangers etc., their relationship with one another, the meaninglessness of their drab lives, forever clouded by the fear of unemployment when the job is finished. But there is one man who works apart from the rest. Frank Owen is an artisan, a master craftsman of restoration that even Mr Sweater, the foreman, can't afford to sack because his skills are rare and essential to bringing the house 'back to life'. He is a socialist and whilst having great compassion for his fellow workers he will nevertheless at times provoke them into examining the wretchedness of their existence. However, it is during a lunch break that Owen, having declared that 'money is the cause of poverty', is provoked by the others into proving his words. This results in the classic scene known as 'The great money trick', a perfect example of the simple economics of that time – depending on one's politics, of course. The book had become a bible among the organized working class of my youth, and one to which I could instinctively relate, having been born and having grown up in an atmosphere of forelock-tugging obeisance and fear of unemployment. So my first venture as a dramatist, whilst not my own original work, performed under my own direction, was deemed a great success, and even came to be regarded as an historic event in the story of Unity Theatre. It was to mark the start of a decade or so of continuing success for me, both as director and writer, at Unity.

I had already flown the parental nest, for the very simple reason that with my growing professional work, spending almost every other hour at Unity, my folks hardly ever saw me, anyway. Also I was twenty-six years of age and my love life, prior to meeting Edith, had become very frustrating. For the sake of respectability I had to show my face at home but found myself so often having to leave a hot maiden in a warm bed in order to catch a cold all-night bus back to the suburbs. My mother, as always, lent a sympathetic ear to my wish to move out. It was my father, she informed me, who had somewhat querulously enquired, 'What does he want to leave home for?'

'Because he's a grown man, now,' she tried to explain patiently.

'That doesn't answer my question,' he responded.

Thinking this somewhat pompous she decided to close the subject with, 'Then I'll have to buy you a book, won't I?'

I had taken a room in a friend's Chelsea flat, which was rather cramped and became even more so when Edith joined me. It was impossible for us both to get out of bed at the same time! We 'lived in sin' until her divorce came through and then we named the day. If my memory serves me correctly it was then that Edith was informed her father had cut her from his will.

The ceremony, in 1946, took place at the Chelsea Register Office, but it wasn't a happy day for the bride, I'm afraid. With the exception of a telegram from her mother, the rest of her family ignored the whole event. Then the friend I had asked to be a witness failed to show up. In a panic I dashed out into the King's Road and grabbed the first person passing by. After I had pleaded my case he reluctantly agreed to stand in. By this time my dear parents were somewhat bewildered. They had had a proper wedding in a church with all the formalities, whilst their son's betrothal had about as much pomp and ceremony as the signing of a pantomime contract with the Grade brothers.

After a lousy lunch my mother and father wished us much happiness and departed. We wandered back to our 'love nest' to be informed by my friend that we had to vacate the room within two weeks as he had sold the flat. I was not surprised when Edith sat down and wept. But within two weeks I had taken out a mortgage, my very first, on a little house near

Hampstead Heath. There were no roses around the door, but who needed roses? I had a family all to myself, it seemed to me, and that was enough.

Another acquisition of mine about this time was an agent – Myron Selznick, one of the most influential in town – and I had come by their invitation. It transpired that David Henley, an agent in the company, acting on the advice of a client, had ventured into the wilds of Somers Town to see me in a revue at Unity Theatre.

The signing of an agent's contract duly took place, only to have David Henley tear it up and drop it into the wastepaper basket. Seeing my surprise he explained, 'If I can't get you the work you deserve, then that's all the contract is worth.' I knew then that I was in good company, and I was to stay with them until they ceased operations in this country.

An appointment was made for me to see Douglass Montgomery. I had already met him during the making of *The Way to the Stars* and he had returned to this country from Hollywood to star in a new play, *Now the Day is Over*, by Charles Freeman and Gerald Savoury, to be presented in London after a short tour. It was a murder mystery with Douglass playing Charlie, the culprit. But now he and the director, Terence de Marney, were faced with the problem of finding a young character actor to play the difficult role of Hughie, described by the authors as a man in his early thirties with the mental capacity of a child of six. It was not the sort of character that one could just slip on like an overcoat and give an audition for just like that. Also, half-wits were thin on the ground in the London contemporary drama scene at that time – although there might have been some critics who disagreed with me! The choice could only be made on the reputation and experience of the actor and I was short on both, but Terence de Marney, who had seen my work at Unity Theatre, convinced Douglass that I was the one for Hughie.

It was a blockbuster on tour and with filmstar Douglass the great attraction, a London theatre had been guaranteed. So it came as a great shock when we all received a five-page, closely typed letter from Douglass, vaguely referring to a conspiracy against him within the Company. It's here in front of me, in the same envelope in which it was delivered to my dressing room forty-six years ago – which was probably the last time I read it. Re-reading it, I find it as confusing, pitiful and harmful as I did then. Confusing because he never gave any indication as to what the conspiracy was or how it manifested itself. Pitiful because he even bothered to remind us of his value at the box office – as if we needed reminding. We had been counting on him to pay our rent for the next few months at least! Harmful because of the demoralizing effect it had on the cast. What was the conspiracy? Who amongst us could have been responsible? We never did find the answer because Douglass ditched the show on the road and returned to Hollywood. And so we went home having lost the London theatre.

Within a few weeks, however, the impresario, Bertie Meyer, decided to present the play, 'on the fringe' as it were, at the Embassy Theatre, Swiss Cottage, with our director, an actor of some status, Terence de Marney, in the role of Charlie. One of the difficulties of playing a part such as Hughie – at times equally difficult for the other actors – is that it is like performing in a vacuum; the character of Lennie in Steinbeck's *Of Mice and Men* poses similar problems. Only characters in close relationship, in Hughie's case his aunt, usually have any mental response. There is also the problem that when performed in the theatre such a character can have, at times, an almost mesmeric effect upon the audience, with their becoming more interested in the half-wit's reaction than to what is actually happening elsewhere on the stage. This was to occur on numerous occasions during my only two but very important scenes, alone with Douglass, when I would gradually become aware of his apparent frustration and anger at times, as he endeavoured to retain his rightful control of the scene.

I am not aware what Douglass's theatrical experience was at that time, but it was only after a few performances with Terry – who was very good as Charlie, but quite different from Montgomery – that it was clear to me how the pace of the play had changed. Terry's character was devoid of the emotional complexities that Douglass had tried to imbue it with, and in consequence of the quickening pace there was less chance for the audience's attention to wander. So I came to the conclusion that there never was a conspiracy at all, but perhaps a conspirator, Hughie, perhaps – through me!

It was over a candle-lit dinner celebrating Edith's thirty-eighth birthday that she said she wanted to have our child. This was a subject we had previously avoided as there had been complications with the birth of my stepdaughter, Zan. Now, however, risk or no risk, she was determined. After receiving the OK from our doctor, we applied ourselves to this pleasurable task with great enthusiasm – but without the desired result. So we went back to our doctor who was most helpful, suggesting various positionings, some of them almost acrobatic; I had never seen Edith from such angles before!

I was even given a tip by a filmstar, who has since become a famous director, who told me that immediately after intercourse his wife did a handstand up against the bedroom wall! Edith drew the line at that. But our doctor was determined (bully for him) and insisted we both take fertility tests.

It was a dull autumn afternoon when I rang the bell of a Harley Street clinic, housed in an ancient building. The door was opened by a laboratory assistant of comparable vintage. She had a nervous chuckle and dithered, so for the purposes of this story I shall refer to her as Miss Dither. She'd been expecting me and I was duly introduced to an aged professor who had slowly emerged from behind some Heath Robinson laboratory equipment. He mumbled some instructions, of which I had been forewarned – my doctor had almost drawn me a diagram! Well, really, masturbation wasn't exactly something new to me. In fact I can remember precisely when and where it began. I was away at camp with the sea cadets, so I was wearing a sailor's suit at the time – not that I think that is entirely relevant, but somebody reported me and the Padre gave me a 'man-to-man' chat. I was all of twelve! But back to Miss Dither. She led me upstairs to a small room which, but for one chair, was devoid of furniture or any kind of decoration whatsoever. Everything was dark brown, including the cell-like window which obviously hadn't been cleaned since war was declared. There was a small, decrepit gas fire which, when lit by Miss Dither, gave out a continuous popping sound. Then, almost with pride, she gave me an odd-shaped glass receptacle. Kept for such occasions? With a knowing smile and a wag of a forefinger she cooed, 'Now do your best for me, Mr Owen.' (I had not long before changed my name.) And leaving me with the echo of an hysterical chuckle, she fled.

It was all so bizarre, and reminded me of Mrs Rottweiler in Newcastle, who'd have no 'hanky-panky' in that hovel she called a guest room. It was difficult enough to imagine sex there, but in that little dark brown room with its hiccuping gas fire, the circumstances were much worse.

But there had to be an end result – even if all I had was 'do-it-yourself'. Later I heard I had passed with flying colours. Edith needed some minor attention and we were soon back upstairs, trying again!

My second production at Unity Theatre was a far cry from *The Ragged Trousered Philanthropists*. It was the first post-war Soviet play to be performed in a foreign country. *The Russian Question*, by Konstantin Simenov was an angry, topical and controversial play about relationships between American and Soviet journalists during the final episodes of the war. On 8 November 1947, the magazine *Illustrated* gave the production a four-page spread and Joan Skipton, in her review, gave her reasons why it had captured the immediate interest of our national press.

> Simenov's latest play is said to have been born at the link-up of the Soviet and American armies at the Elbe. With two colleagues he was interviewed by the British and American press. Some launched a merciless bombardment of questions a British reporter has called vicious and tendentious. 'I must do more about this,' declared Simenov angrily. He kept his word in *The Russian Question*, whose many broadsides at the American press tactics include a swift crack about some Russian newsmen who found a New York lunch in their honour turned into a press conference.

Miss Skipton went on to say that I 'polished up the production' and to remark that 'there were six ambassadors present on the opening night'. The main thing I remember is a very heavy session with the Soviet Cultural Attaché, a determined lady who rejected out of hand my suggestions to help underline the human emotions of the play. I explained, pleaded and argued, but the lady was adamant. She had given Unity Theatre permission to do the play on the strict understanding that there were to be no alterations whatsoever, and as far as I can recall there weren't. Well, maybe just a few.

Naturally, the right-wing press were not amused. Even the *News Chronicle* took to political moralizing with '... if Mr Simenov had kept his temper he would have written a more significant play.' He might well have, but I think he had every right to be angry. His country had withstood the full onslaught of the Nazi war machine at a cost of twenty million lives.

But there was no doubt it had been a triumph for Unity and all who were concerned in its production, which included Edith, making her début with the Unity Players in an excellent portrayal of Jessie, the wife of a victimized American journalist. This was not, let me hasten to add, from any social or political conviction, but simply her attempt to follow the old-fashioned maxim that it helped a marriage if a wife tried to share her husband's interests. She was also a frustrated actress, which might have been the real reason!

Not long afterwards – the very morning that Edith got back from hospital, excitedly declaring herself 'preggers' – I received a script of the Victorian comedy *Caste* by Tom Robertson, with the offer of the role of Sam Gerridge. It came through Kitty Black, Assistant Administrator of the Company of Four, headed by Binkie Beaumont at the Lyric Theatre, Hammersmith, where it would be produced. It was to prove to be the turning point in my career.

Caste has now become a classic. Hartnell, in his *Oxford Companion to the Theatre*, refers to it thus: '... Robertson founded what has been called "the cup and saucer drama" – that is the drama of the realistic, contemporary, domestic interior. His nouns were recognizable, his dialogue credible, his plots, though they now seem somewhat artificial, were true to his time, and an immense advance on anything that had gone before.'

It was a perfect comedy for a post-war 'pick-me-up', and most assuredly proved to be so, particularly for me. The role of Sam Gerridge fitted me like a glove and was light-years away from 'Hughie'. Sam, a chirpy young Cockney plumber, along with his sweetheart Polly, played by Brenda Bruce, became the 'comedy duo' of that season. The cast abounded with 'theatre names', including Elliot Mason, Frith Banbury, Morland Graham, Clem McCallin and Iris Russell. Directed by Peter Ashmore, it was an immediate success and after our scheduled run at the Lyric we were sent out on a brief tour whilst arrangements were made for us to return to the West End. Both Brenda and Elliot had prior commitments and were replaced by Diana Churchill and Marie Lohr for the opening at the Comedy Theatre.

That opening night in the West End was my first taste of the magic, the audience that won't let you go, the flowers, the kissing, the tears. The famous – and others – crowding into one's dressing room (matchbox size, on the top floor and next to the water cistern), meeting their friends and staying to chat making it impossible to get out of costume, a total stranger offering champagne in a tooth mug saying, 'Well done, old boy, hope it's your beaker!' And, finally, David Henley taking Edith and me to the Savoy Grill after the show. Me standing next to the well-known agent, Al Parker, in the gents, as he informs me, 'You're a hot potato tonight,' then, adjusting his dress, 'Remember me if you want to be a big star,' then exiting. I assumed he was talking to me, it was rather dark in there. It's also a conversation I'll never forget for another reason: it was the first time I had ever been expected to leave a tip for having a pee!

I think it was the sentimental attachment to *Caste* that enthused me, years later, to adapt it as a musical, writing the lyrics to Ronnie Hill's music. According to the programme I also choreographed and directed the musical numbers and played my original role of Sam, to which my father's only observation was, 'Are you also playing in the orchestra?'

The musical was premièred in October 1955 at the Theatre Royal, Windsor, with a cast that included Leslie Henson, Betty Paul and Sara Gregory. Oscar Lewenstein was sufficiently impressed to take an option but could do nothing further after another musical version of the same play had slipped into the West End and had proved a disaster. It was a few years later, in discussion with my dear friend Denis Martin, who was then managing the Players Theatre, that I suggested our musical version of *Caste* as an ideal show for the Players, and he asked to hear the songs. Straight away I rang Ronnie Hill with the good news which was brought to an abrupt halt when he informed me that, in a fit of deep depression, he had destroyed every piece of music he had ever written.

One morning I was called for an interview with Mr Raoul Walsh, an American film director who was holding court at his Mayfair Hotel suite. Ushered in by some minion, I saw him sitting to the right of the room, as I thought, so walked over to meet him and straight into a mirror that covered the entire wall! Now, I have experienced mirrored ceilings and once I was told of a mirror covered floor, but I failed, at the time, to see the use of a mirrored wall, other than for giving me one nasty headache!

He wore a black eye-patch and should have added a black hat and parrot the way I was feeling, but I could have been bleeding to death for all Mr Walsh cared. He didn't even bother to look up from his scribbling. But I'd had many an interview with these film people from 'God's Own Country' and could anticipate his reaction as he looked at me. I could imagine him saying, 'Oh, shit, not another one! Why do they keep sending me these peculiar people? This guy doesn't even *look* like an actor!' Meanwhile, I reciprocated with a studied look of boredom which I hoped he'd interpret as 'I don't care if I get the job or not and furthermore, don't ask me to sit down, you ignorant bastard.' He didn't, so you see we were of one accord, except I still had a nasty headache.

However, it was quite extraordinary how quickly it disappeared when I arrived home to the message that my agent wished me to phone him.

The news was that J Arthur Rank were offering me a film contract and would I care to drop by sometime so that we might discuss the matter? It all sounded so casual, 'drop by sometime'. Hey, I'm being offered a film contract, what was there to discuss? I dropped by immediately!

Cecil Tennant was practising his golf swing with a walking stick as I was ushered into his office, seated, then given a cup of coffee by his secretary. This was 'Mr Big' of the Myron Selznick (British) Operations. And when I say 'big' I'm telling no lie. He must have stood nearly seven foot in his socks. Mark you, when I am seated on one of those low settees, everyone looks seven foot tall!

He introduced himself, still swinging, and it wouldn't have surprised me if his secretary had shouted 'Fore'! Everything was so casual, the entire office staff so blasé, no one seemed at all excited or concerned that I had been offered a film contract. Well, no one but myself, that is. As I recall, I became rather piqued as the golf practice continued with no more than mundane pleasantries being exchanged – even the secretary threw in her ha'pennyworth as she busied herself. It was like a well-rehearsed sketch and I was the only one who didn't know my lines. But film contracts, and excited apprentices with stars in their eyes, were meat and drink to Myron Selznick. He had artistes that earned more in a day than I would earn in a year with my Rank contract. But Cecil Tennant evidently considered mine a special case.

'You don't really want to sign a film contract, do you?' he asked.

'Yes, I do,' was my immediate rejoinder.

He stopped the golf practice and his secretary returned to her office. He then began to explain why he didn't think it such a good idea for me personally, at the present time. 'Why sign a film contract? There are plenty of films being made and plenty of good parts to go with them.' This was true, we had a flourishing film industry with a growing number of major production companies, including Rank.

And Rank, as Cecil went on to say, 'Already has one hundred and fifty contract artists of which ninety per cent are stereo-typed, tall, well-chiselled leading men – which you are not, William, let's face it. So where are you going to fit into all this?'

I didn't take Cecil Tennant's advice, but I shall always remember his final words as I left his office. 'You have a rare theatrical talent and should you become a leading film actor, it will be because of your reputation in the theatre.'

However, my personal experience has led me to the conclusion that no matter how good the film or the role may be, when the talk is of filmstars we are speaking of that indefinable quality that only the camera can discover. You've either got it or you haven't, 'it' being defined as whether the camera loves you or not. With all the many, many films in which I have appeared, I have never felt my relationship with the camera anything more than platonic.

4

And the Owens Begat

Not once during my teenage years of Lew Stone, double-breasted waistcoats, padded shoulders, winklepickers, acne and Brylcreem did I imagine that, in spite of my father's Marxist teachings, I would, someday, own a Rolls-Royce – a name now demoted to 'Roller' by the uninitiated and 'yuppytongued'. But towards the end of the 1940s I was to become, paradoxically, the proud, but shamefaced possessor of a streamlined 1936 beauty. I am looking at a photograph of her now, she had to be female, of course – what a figure! And such upholstery! Today a Roller means nothing, any chairman of a privatized utility probably runs at least two, but in 1947 it was something spoken of in awe, a dream of perfection and reserved for the rich and privileged.

Well, I am neither rich nor privileged, but when, suddenly and due to circumstances unimaginable today, I was faced with actually having to own a car, I can only shake my head at the unreality of the idea of owning a Rolls-Royce, a prospect which seems both ludicrous and frankly unacceptable. I would add that although it became necessary to have one, a car has never been a must in my life. My idea of doing nothing is when some joker suggests 'a ride in the car'.

When I played 'bit parts' in movies, and when such work took me to Pinewood Studios, I travelled by train to Uxbridge and then caught a bus which, for an eight o'clock call, meant

51

leaving home at 6 a.m. For my return I had a foolproof system – linger around the car park and someone would be sure to offer you a lift back to town. I can remember many such a ride with very illustrious chauffeurs, such as Lord Olivier and Douglas Fairbanks Junior.

With the signing of the film contract, and having been cast for my first starring role with Patricia Roc in a film called *When the Bough Breaks*, there was a sudden demand for my presence at Pinewood, making travelling by train and bus impossible. I just had to have a car. But how? Where from? This was 1947, cars were generally conspicuous by their absence – one could actually breathe in London in those days. There wasn't a car being produced anywhere in the country at that time. My only chance was to find a garage that might have one 'in mothballs', preserved for the duration of the war. Well, after what could best be likened to a Mafia operation, I was put in touch with a garage that had two. One, a clapped-out Ford that wouldn't have made it to the breakers' yard under its own steam and the second a 1936 Rolls-Royce for £2,000. How such a price would relate in today's market, I don't know, but it was damned high for 1947! However, HP terms – something my father would have described as 'the vice of the working class' – were available. Over our evening meal, I explained my dilemma to Edith. Her immediate reaction was, 'Buy the Rolls-Royce!' I protested on economic grounds. She retaliated with, 'You've got to have a car – this is an investment!' She always sounded so logical when we were in love. I bought the Rolls-Royce on the 'never-never'.

Then came the day all preparations were over; the pre-publicity, the grooming, the make-up and the camera test. All the measurements had been taken and materials chosen for my wardrobe (far too expensive for the character I was playing – a corner-shop grocer). For the first time I was dressed on the ground floor of Bermans, the theatrical costumiers, instead of in the basement with the peasants –

where I often ended up wearing Dickie Attenborough's cast-offs!

With all this attention my imagination was running riot. The studio where the film was to be made hadn't yet been named, but I figured it had to be Pinewood. Star Dressing Room No. 2! Right next door to the beautiful Patricia Roc, me her leading man, she my first leading lady! Patricia was an inch or so taller than me so I had to wear lifts in my shoes – so what, look what they did for Alan Ladd. My name would be on the door, just under that star! It was all going to be luxurious. I didn't speak from any previous experience, of course. Until then a dressing room meant sharing with others. Sometimes I might have the odd one to myself, usually the size of a broom cupboard, with the loo at the end of the corridor. But not now, Billy Boy. No doubt some minion would call to enquire if I preferred lunch in my room or should a reservation be made in the restaurant? Before, I had always eaten in the canteen – I knew my place! But there had been some changes made and I would now eat in the restaurant, call in the bar on the way, say hello, buy a drink or two, maybe. But before I sat down to eat I'd have a few words with my friend Frank Godwin at the High Executive Table. Of course, no one knew he and I had performed and written shows together at Unity Theatre. A little star-gazing, but this was it. This was the way it was going to be from now on. Of course, space would be reserved in the car park for my Rolls-Royce! In the event, it turned out that all my imaginings were just that: purely imaginary! This is something I have experienced often in life, and led me to my personal motto, 'Always anticipate the worst, anything better is then a bonus.'

When the Bough Breaks was not made at Pinewood. Instead the old Gainsborough Studios in Islington were re-opened. They could be likened to a rabbit warren, with dressing rooms to match. London was frozen to a standstill, there was a national fuel shortage and, owing to rationing of power the only means of studio lighting and heating came from an aged generator parked in the street outside. We never used our dressing rooms, they were too cold. There was a one-bar fire in the studio which artistes were supposed to share – if they could squeeze past Patricia and me. As for the catering, I remember nothing and perhaps it's just as well – but we did seem to drink a lot of unsweetened cocoa!

In those days there was the natural assumption of status that went with owning a Rolls-Royce. For instance, I made a film called *The Girl Who Couldn't Quite* and, before there are any misconceptions, I should explain that the plot concerned the inability of a young girl to smile and how I, as a tramp, wandered into her life and cured her. One morning driving the Rolls from the studio to a nearby location, all ready in tramp costume and make-up, I was waved down by a police car. Having already given my views on the automobile generally, I would also add that I never derived any excitement or experienced any macho feelings in driving at excessive speed, but this aspiring 'Inspector Morse' wasn't to be deterred. He asked to see my licence. Of course I'd left all my particulars back at the studio, but I was saved any tedious explanation when the other arm of the law exclaimed:

'Oh, Christ, it's 'im!'

'Oo?'

'You know – what's 'is name – you know.'

'I don't know, Fred, that's why I'm askin' yer.'

''E's on the films – 'e was in that one about war – what's it called – you know!'

As I was in a hurry I told them my name. Now began comic policeman banter as they studied my clothes.

'Fings not going too well then, are they?'

Haw! Haw! Haw!

'Poor old sod, 'ere, get yerself a cuppa tea.'

Ha! Ha! Ha!

I think that was the only time I was recognized in that Rolls-Royce – dressed as a tramp. My Roller spent most of its time parked outside Unity Theatre, which caused a few raised eyebrows among the Party members!

With the completion in 1947 of *When the Bough Breaks*, my first film under contract, so began the pressure for me to change my name before its distribution. The main source of complaint stemmed from the United States where the distributors just would not believe that anyone could be born with a 'handle' such as Rowbotham, and felt it could have an adverse effect on my 'box-office potential'. My first reaction was to refuse on principle. 'What's good enough for my father, etc. etc.' However, after an excellent dinner with Sydney Box, the producer, who, plying me with brandy, explained the logic and dire necessity of not upsetting the Americans, I relented and became Bill Owen, using my first and third Christian names. Legally my family remain Rowbothams, but for an actor I think Sydney was right. It's neat, tidy and easy to remember.

The film had a mixed press reception, being described by some as 'a weepie'. It was about a woman who has an illegitimate baby which she is forced to hand over to a rich, childless couple; then, having married me, wants the child back again. I can't remember whether there was supposed to be something wrong with me. I have to admit it wasn't quite my scene, as a critic confirmed – 'Bill Owen must be as surprised as we are to find himself playing a romantic lead.' It is a fact, I've never kissed a woman passionately in a film in my life, and only once on stage – and that was in a play I wrote myself!

Then came the usual publicity jamboree, travelling around the country selling the film and, because of my experience in variety as a solo entertainer, I found myself in great demand, particularly in front of cinema audiences.

To walk out on to the stage of one of the giant Odeon or Granada cinemas could be an awesome experience, especially when, having reached the microphone, all you could do was make 'jolly banter' about a film the audience had paid good money for and were waiting impatiently to see!

I can remember accompanying one Rank starlet who had done rather well in her first film. She stood on the vast stage of the Troxy, Mile End, joyfully prattling away to a stony silence which was finally broken by a voice booming out of the darkness, 'Why don'tcha piss off!' Collapse of young party!

To Edith and me 'a son was born' on 8 April 1949. I shall never forget that moment when my father held his grandson for the first time, saying with tears in his eyes, 'Well, that's another Bill in the family.' This wasn't presumption on his part. Naming the first male child after the father was long a tradition with working-class people. Nevertheless, mother, ever tactful, remarked, 'He's like his mother.'

Edith had come through it surprisingly well, and it was to be a few years later before I learned from a specialist of the risk she had taken by having another child. But she was happy, there had been flowers and congratulations from her parents with an invitation for us to visit them as soon as she was fit enough.

It was just prior to a visit to her family in Glasgow that Edith asked me if I could forgo the family tradition of naming the first son after his father and have him called Thomas after her father. The phrase she used was 'as a peace offering'. This was, as I recall, a reference to their last altercation when she had stormed out of the house, for good, to join me.

So it seemed I was already involved in this rather turbulent relationship before I had even met her father. But I agreed, kidding myself it was my duty to try and help heal the family rift, which, I should add did nothing for my father's bitter disappointment.

We were met at the station by a chauffeur-driven limousine and a nanny, hired specially for the occasion, who immediately took charge of little Tom. The house was one of those granite fortress-like buildings that were the hallmark of the well-to-do of Glasgow suburbia. It stood in its own grounds, a quarter of an acre or so, with a pebble drive leading to a rather forbidding front door. A maid answered the bell almost before Edith had rung it and there waiting to welcome us were Mr and Mrs Stevenson, my first and very own in-laws! But it was the 'bairn' that stole the limelight; wee Tommy, the first male child to be born to the Stevenson clan! The large hallway rang with 'Ooohs' and 'Ahhhs', 'What a bonny lad', etc., etc. As I recall, my only pressing concern at the moment was to find the lavatory, but in such new circumstances I felt a certain embarrassment as to how to address the question, and to whom.

Whether old Tom was trying to make some point or other when he invited me along to the Ayr races a couple of days later, I don't know, but I accepted readily. I had never been to a race meeting before and here I was son-in-law to a man held in high esteem by Scotland's racing fraternity. This became apparent from the moment we arrived. He knew everyone and everyone knew him, in the enclosure, the parade ring, even in the weighing-in room. And on he strolled, doffing his grey Derby, occasionally stopping to talk with other owners. Some of the ragged arsed punters almost touched their forelocks in deference. Whether or not this was in anticipation of his obligingly 'marking their cards' I can't say but if so they were to be disappointed. This was to become a bone of contention between us, and very soon.

Edith had previously warned me that he disliked any member of his family 'having a flutter', with himself the exception, of course. I didn't take this seriously and as the time for the first race drew near, and being totally inexperienced, I asked him how I went about placing a bet. 'Ye'll nae lose your money whilst ye're wi' me,' he replied. In view of the circumstances, I would probably have gone along with this one and just wandered away to back the favourite. But right or wrong I felt this old man was handing me a challenge, staking a claim; Edith might be my wife but she was also his daughter! This was something I was to be reminded of many times during my marriage to Edith. I accepted the challenge. 'Look, Mr Stevenson, I'm going to have a bet whether you like it or not,' I replied. 'Now, either you will give me some advice or I'll go to the bookmaker like a lamb to slaughter.' I had picked up the gauntlet, we levelled with one another. He eventually took my card and marked it. I won four races out of a possible six – total winnings, eighteen pounds! From then on our relationship could best be described as formal.

Whatever the Rank front office envisaged regarding *When the Bough Breaks* and what it could do for me and vice-versa, my judgement is that they were disappointed for us both. Sydney Box stated to the press that I '... was a coming star of tomorrow.' But I was already beginning to worry about today. There was always the danger of believing one's own publicity and I had a gut feeling of foreboding, not helped by recalling my agent's words – 'You don't want to sign a film contract, do you?' But I did! And now I had one, but the hard fact was, as I would soon learn, no one knew quite what to do with me. I didn't seem to fit into any particular category. I wasn't tall and could hardly be described as handsome. Unfortunately, the anti-hero had yet to be discovered; quite a few years would pass before a young man, son of a Manchester bookmaker would hit the screen with *Saturday Night and Sunday Morning*.

Whilst kicking my heels I received an invitation to return to the St Martin's Theatre in a musical revue called *Sugar and Spice*, my co-star being the well known comedienne, Ethel Revnell. So I decided to exercise my option of playing in the theatre when not being used in a film. At least, I comforted myself, I knew what I was doing 'on the boards' – or so I thought. The doubts began to creep in after the opening number on the first night. I'll never forget that song, it was called 'This is a Happy Event for Someone', a sort of congratulatory piece for the birth in November 1948 of Prince Charles. The first scene had a woodland setting with a chorus of young singers and dancers all dressed as toys – bunnies, golliwogs and teddy bears. As their routine ended, the scene changed to one of a nursery and I, dressed as a stork, wings and all, had to fly in, singing the opening number. When I'd concluded, Ethel, a very tall lady, was to have been pushed on stage, dressed as a baby and sitting in a pram the size of a small caravan. She then went into her routine. Now, when I say I was going to fly in, I *mean* fly in, wings flapping and legs outstretched for a two-point (if lucky) landing. I sat up in the rafters above the stage – the 'flies' – and, fitted with the famous 'Kirby Flying Harness', was meant to float down gently to the footlights, still singing. Sounds good, doesn't it? Well, as Robert Burns very nearly said, the best laid schemes of management an' men gang aft a-gley.

Sitting on my lofty perch I looked down in amazement as all hell broke loose below owing to the woodland setting giving way (literally) to the nursery scene. What should have gone up came down and vice-versa. Ropes became entangled, taking with them the odd stagehand or two, their language rising loud and profane above the efforts of the orchestra which was playing furiously and for the twelfth time my introduction to 'This is a Happy Event for Someone'. Perceptively, it occurred to me that if I wanted to see my family again, discretion was the better part of valour. From now on I'd fly British Airways. I made my entrance from the side of the stage.

The journey from the flies to the stage was not one that I, as an actor, was used to making. Consequently I was rather late in making my entrance. They had in fact started without me, skipping my song entirely. Ethel, now in the middle of her 'baby' number said as I appeared, a rather bedraggled stork, 'You're late, I've been born for ten minutes!' But the show did settle down, sinking entirely after three weeks!

Not long after, a very excited Mick Manning, general secretary at Unity Theatre, called me about a new Soviet comedy that had just arrived from Moscow entitled *The Whole World Over*

by Konstantin Simenov. Now I had had enough experience of
plays and playwrights, certainly in this country, never to dub
them definitively as either dramatic or comedic. For starters,
the Bard himself had done well enough with an amalgam of
both. Mind you, he never had to write about a war where
twenty million people were sacrificed. However, this once I
had to admit to doubt, that the playwright, who had thundered
his way through *The Russian Question* with such rage and
anger would follow it with what was described as a 'delightful
comedy'. I read it, I was wrong, it was – and more! Mick and
I met for lunch to discuss an immediate production while I
was still waiting for the phone to ring. Lunch, as usual, was
next door to the theatre at the London, Midland and Scottish
Railway Carters and Draymens Café. Meat and two veg,
spotted dick and custard and a large tea – now up to one
shilling and fourpence! But to hell with the expense, it was
handy and I could keep an eye on the Roller parked outside.

The Whole World Over was a delight and it was hard to
believe that this warm and tender comedy about a Russian family
trying to pick up the peace after the horrors of war had been
written by the same man who had thundered out his anger in *The
Russian Question*. It was a good production with an excellent set
by the Amorals, my ever-faithful designers, and a cast that I
doubt could have been bettered, including Edith playing a
returning army surgeon. What notices there were were excellent – the absence of the 'Nationals' was obviously due to the
slamming they got during *The Russian Question*.

During the run there was an unannounced visit from Beverly
Baxter, Tory MP and eminent critic of the *Evening Standard*,
whose presence had remained undetected until a review
appeared the next day.

Let me [Mr Baxter wrote] confess that I journeyed this week
to the terra incognita which lies a mile north of St Pancras
Station and went to the Unity Theatre which is pink to red
in politics.

What is more, I saw a comedy written by Konstantin Simenov who wrote another play, *The Russian Question*, in which he was rude to America and particularly American reporters. The present offering, now nearing the end of its run, is called *The Whole World Over*, dealing with the adventure of a Moscow household at the close of the war.

... This fellow Simenov has such a sure gift of comedy and yet such a keen sense of values ... One can see the influence of Dickens and of Chekhov in his writing. It is warm, full-blooded and richly humorous, the entire cast are amateurs who work during the day in office or factory. Yet they give a surprisingly satisfactory performance, and I am grateful to them for an evening of rare delight.

No doubt because of his grandson, and in consequence the easing of the relationship between me and Edith, old Tom restored his daughter's private income. Then, to my great surprise, my Rank contract was renewed. As it was coming up to our wedding anniversary, Edith decided the treat was on her and we would celebrate at the Caprice. This was the 'in place' for anyone who was anybody in showbiz. Over coffee she handed me an envelope containing a cheque for £1,000 and a note which read, 'Happy Anniversary, Darling. Why not invest on the merry-go-round for the next year? My love.' I was speechless at such generosity, almost to the point of embarrassment, and I admitted to being somewhat confused as to its purpose. As always, she came straight to the point. She already had doubts about the film contract. Quoting a publicity blurb, she continued, 'If you are to be the British James Cagney, why don't they give you the roles, and if they aren't to be found, have them written?' I pointed out that this wasn't Hollywood and there were probably many actors under contract to Rank with a similar beef. But she was not to be deterred. If they wouldn't make things happen, then we must try. Looking around the restaurant she said, 'We'll join the merry-go-round. We will invest that money for a year being seen in the right places at the right time with the right people. I will accompany you and arrange everything!' I looked around the restaurant and recognized many well-known faces, and many unknowns doing their damnest trying to be recognized.

I have never forgiven myself for my thoughtless response to her loving concern for me. 'My dear,' I said, 'don't waste your money.' We didn't exchange a word until we got home. Then we had a flaming row, our first since we had known each other. I made attempts to defend my attitude. I wasn't very good at the social scene, it doesn't come easily to me, even after all these years. I envy those who, even as perfect strangers, are able to introduce themselves, join an existing conversation, be at ease and find themselves immediately accepted. Unfortunately, I have the habit of appearing rather aloof on such occasions. I collect my drink and seek out some niche or corner where I stand as if waiting for a bus. For example, in my capacity as Chairman of Arts for Labour, an organization of professional artists supporting the Labour Party, I was recently invited to a shindig at the House of Commons where I took up such a stance. After about forty minutes, having spoken to no one other than having a brief exchange with John Smith, I quietly slipped away. So, I still try to defend myself against the 'merry-go-round', such a charade would do nothing for me. All I could count on then, as now, was my talent.

'Nothing will count with you,' said Edith, 'until you get that working-class chip off your shoulder. You're not working class any more. You earn four thousand pounds a year. It's your father who still has to drive the trolley bus.' So investment in the merry-go-round never took place. But for the sake of our future relationship I should have been honest with Edith and given my true reason once and for all. I didn't need or want her father's money to influence my career – or my family for that matter.

5

The Big Apple?

Beverly Baxter had responded to an invitation from Unity Theatre to attend the opening of *What's Left?*, a political satire written by Geoffrey Parsons, Berkeley Fase and Roger Woddis, and produced by yours truly. I accorded myself the duty of welcoming him and conducting him to his seat. As the overture had already begun, our conversation was brief, but his closing comment has mystified me to this day, 'Bill, there will be no more,' he said.

Now, I accept the fact that I do have a tendency to over-dramatize, as has been pointed out to me by directors on occasions, but what lay behind this odd remark? More of what? Had it evolved from his very favourable review of *The Whole World Over*? Had the *Standard* or Tory Central Office lodged a complaint? Publicity for such a show and such a theatre in a right-wing newspaper was rare. But I had never imagined Unity as being a big enough fish politically to warrant such attention; then again, my journey to America a few months later was also to have unexplained personal reper-cussions.

Once again, however, Mr Baxter gave *What's Left?* a rave review headed, 'Unfair to the Tories – but how I laughed' and concluding with '... but let us keep politics out of our verdict and praise this revue for being a thoroughly professional job and very nearly the funniest thing in London'. He remained on our VIP first-night invitation list until he died, but he never came again.

Michael Benthall, a well-known theatre director, told me he had just returned from America and was crossing Leicester Square when he saw my photograph, among others, outside the Leicester Square cinema, advertising a film: *Trottie True*. This was a piece of Edwardian whimsy about a comic music-hall act. Jean Kent played the name part with Hattie Jacques and I completing the partnership. The story involved rich stage-door johnnies, romance, wealth, misunderstanding and a happy ending.

It was seeing the photograph that gave him the idea of phoning my agent to enquire if I might be interested in playing Touchstone in *As You Like It*, presented by the New York Theater Guild starring Katharine Hepburn as Rosalind. It was to open in the late autumn of 1949 with a tour prior to a short season on Broadway. Well, I wasn't interested. I was enjoying family life and revelling in my new role as father. Furthermore, I had no experience whatsoever of classical theatre.

Since our difference of opinion (to put it mildly) and my refusal of the offer to be seen 'in the right places', there had been very little discussion between Edith and I regarding my work, but this sudden American offer seemed to re-awaken her interest and faith in me, thank heavens! She vigorously remonstrated with me over my negative attitude, while at the same time breast-feeding Tommy, as a result of which he kept losing her nipple, which did not please him. However, regardless of her son's annoyance and frustration, she managed to convince me that I should at least see Michael Benthall to discuss the matter.

During our meeting, he told me that in his endeavour to cast the role of Touchstone, he 'must have met every top comedian in America – including Buster Keaton'. He went on to ask me if I had seen the play. I told him just once and I hadn't been impressed. As an afterthought I felt I should add it was the Sir Donald Wolfit Company. He smiled as he commented, 'Not a band of actors renowned for their ensemble playing. How was Touchstone? 'Very old,' I replied, then compensated by adding that it had been during the war when there had been a shortage of everything, even actors.

He was aware of my total lack of experience in the classical theatre, but this was, he pointed out, his exact reason for choosing me. 'I want you to discover how to play Touchstone,' he said. With that he made me promise to give him my answer within twenty-four hours and we parted company. That evening I received a further lecture from Edith. I signed the contract. I would be away for the duration of the play's run, with a proviso from Rank that should I be needed for a movie I would be released at once.

My flight to New York was booked for the last week of October 1949. It was this flight, my first, that was to determine my resolve never to journey by aeroplane again, unless my work demanded. It had been preceded by a morning of panic when I had informed Cecil Tennant, who was responsible for my journey, that despite my following to the letter all the necessary procedures, the American Embassy had failed to send my visa, without which, I had been informed, there was no point in making the trip. Thankfully, the necessary paperwork turned up in the nick of time.

The moment I boarded the plane, *not* going on the trip struck me as being an excellent idea. I was confronted with a gloomy interior, uncomfortable seats, no service – not even a drink – and, worse, it was crammed to the doors with elderly European refugees who, like me, seemed to be flying for the first time. However, they had an edge on me, they were able to seek solace and safety through faith and prayer – the latter to a degree of decibels and non-stop for the entire journey! Because the plane couldn't reach America in one hop, we flew to Shannon, refuelled, then kept everything crossed over the Atlantic in the hope we would reach Goose Bay where, once again, we were to take on more fuel in order to fly down to New York.

Never has the sight of mother earth been so welcome as when that plane touched down at Idlewild Airport. The feeling of terra firma beneath my feet almost persuaded me to kneel and kiss the tarmac. However, my joy was short-lived when I was confronted by the Customs official who examined my documents.

He wore that bland, uninterested expression that seems to go with the uniform. Suddenly his whole demeanour changed as he examined my visa. I immediately had the feeling that I was about to be interrogated. I wasn't far wrong. 'If you say you're here to act, what proof have you?' I had no idea. 'You say you're gonna tour with this show – where? What cities?' Again, I had no answer. And so it went on, until he asked, 'What are you gonna do when this show folds?' I grabbed the opportunity, leant across the counter and whispered, 'Effing well go home!' For the first time we seemed to strike common ground – I'd spoken his language. He stamped my documents and I passed through the barrier, having been 'welcomed' to the land that God continually blesses! I examined my visa for any indication or reference to my character, there was nothing as far as I could see.

However, I was welcomed to the Algonquin Hotel, famed for its showbiz clientele where, it is said, bad notices for a show could empty the supper room in a flash! But the welcome didn't last long when I discovered that I could only afford the room – eating was out of the question!

I promptly removed myself to a dump on 7th Avenue called the Wellington and found myself in a room like a broom cupboard! They really made you feel welcome there. Going into the barber's shop for a much-needed haircut, I was greeted by the assistant refusing to cut it because it was too long! I agreed, but pointed out that that was the reason for coming to the barber's, wasn't it? So he turned nasty. 'I don't wanna cut your hair – OK?'

On my second day, I was informed that rehearsals would not commence for three weeks to a month – which they must have known before I left London!

The prospect of a month in New York, on a tight budget, knowing no one, was something I wasn't looking forward to, so I rang the only man I knew in America.

I had first met John Metzler during the war when he was a GI stationed in the north of Scotland and I was playing Gunner Cohen in *Mr Bolfry*. We had met in a bar in Aberdeen. I remember we talked a lot, but then we always talked a lot, right through our friendship, always putting the world to rights. Now, in the autumn of 1949, he was back at school, teaching in his home town of Bradford, Pennsylvania. I had written telling him of my visit to the States and now, hearing of my plight, he insisted on coming to New York at once and taking me back to stay with him and his dear wife, Lee.

Bradford, Pennsylvania was a typical small friendly American town with a main street, a hotel, high school and folk simply taking their time. They pumped a little oil, mined some coal, and were very proud of the fact that the world-famous Zippo cigarette lighter issued, I believe, to all US forces during the war, was made in Bradford.

There weren't many visitors from England and they made me very welcome; for a few weeks I became one of them. John insisted I take some drama classes at the high school. I spoke to the Quakers about our still present restrictions back home. The mention of food rationing immediately prompted the response, 'Should we send food parcels?' People would say, 'Mornin'' when I walked along the High Street; it was light-years away from the indifference of New York. And so, when the time came for me to return, there were many folk who shook their heads in sympathy.

At last came the first day of rehearsal, where I was to meet the company of actors, all of whom were total strangers to me – except Kate Hepburn, my adult screen love. She who had taken over from all that relentless wrestling in the back row of the local Odeon, making me pay attention to what was happening on the screen.

It all began in my Sea Cadet period with the dewy-eyed

Sylvia Sidney and the voluptuous Ethel Waters. Then came Myrna Loy and sophistication. I started carrying an umbrella and wore a double-breasted waistcoat, whilst my mother complained about the state of my underwear – 'Supposing you got run over!' Then I grew up, and there was Kate. And there she was that first morning – for real, with all my illusions safe and sound.

She introduced me to my fellow actors, including, to my surprise, another guest actor from England, Ernest Thesiger, who was to play Jaques. Kate informed me confidentially that he was a master of petit point and had often practised with Queen Mary. We very soon discovered that he and I had very little in common. In fact I can only recall our ever having one conversation, which took place as we accompanied each other across Boston Common in the small hours after a party. It was at this social gathering that Kate introduced me to Spencer Tracy, in whose presence I always thought she behaved rather like an adolescent schoolgirl, or was I jealous? She worshipped him, as is clear from her recent autobiography: 'I have no idea how Spencer felt about me. I can only say that if he hadn't liked me he wouldn't have hung around ... We just passed twenty-seven years together in what was to be absolute bliss. It's called LOVE.'

We talked, well, Kate talked and I did my best, but Spencer made no effort whatsoever, not a word. Then, apparently bored, he suddenly rose, turned to me and said, 'You know your business,' and joined some friends.

Rehearsals did not begin well with my concept of Touchstone as a raunchy clown, an opinion shared by an unseen audience judging by the sighs of remorse and stage whispers emanating from the gloom of the auditorium of the theatre in which we were rehearsing. I particularly remember Act III, scene 3 where, in the forest, Touchstone tries to persuade Audrey, an innocent country wench, that her ignorance is a virtue. She prays that the gods will make her honest, to which Touchstone replies, 'Truly, and to cast away honesty on a foul slut, were to put good meat into an unclean dish', saying which I slapped her inner thigh. This almost brought on apoplexy somewhere in the stalls the first time I tried it.

Kate was most receptive to any ideas I might have during rehearsal, but they were frowned upon by her drama adviser, Constance Collier. The other unseen voices were those of the New York Theater Guild management. Theresa Helburn, Lawrence Langner and I began to lose faith in me, which made rehearsals as far as I was concerned a waste of time. After rehearsals the director came to me and expressed the management's doubts over my interpretation of the role. We went back to my hotel and after a couple of drinks, or perhaps more than a couple, I learned that *he* was being 'told' how to direct the play. I laid my cards on the table: either he was going to make his own suggestions or *I* would continue to try to find the way to play Touchstone – and without the assistance of an uninvited audience. I then saw that he'd fallen asleep. 'I'm waiting for an answer!' I yelled. He was immediately awake and, rising slowly, he unsteadily made his way to the bar, ordered more drinks and proclaimed to the barman, 'Let them go and shit – you play it as you want, do you hear!' He then tottered out to find a taxi. The barman turned to me in astonishment, the first time I'd seen a human reaction from any member of the hotel staff. 'Don't drink on an empty stomach,' I warned. 'Particularly after a sticky rehearsal.' Then I staggered off to bed.

I had one further 'rub' with the New York Theater Guild during the New York run, which occurred when Kate was ordered to bed with a mild flu.

Whilst a fully rehearsed understudy was ready to perform, the Guild felt, probably quite rightly, that without Kate the patrons who had booked in advance would demand their money back, resulting in an immediate drop in attendance and possibly jeopardizing the future of the show. So they closed the play temporarily, only for a few days as it turned out, but it was then we were informed that everyone connected with the show would be paid during the closure – with the exception of the actors. I just could not believe this. Of all the people that might be essential to the curtain rising, surely the most important and indispensable were the actors – irrespective of the star! Whilst the attitude of the rest of the company seemed to be one of reluctant acceptance and resignation, I immediately sought out the company manager. I protested vehemently that I considered it a gross insult that the actors alone should be meted out such treatment and that the British Actors' Equity Association would never have agreed to such a state of affairs. He then informed me that I had signed an American Equity contract and whilst I continued to be employed in the States I would abide by the rules; furthermore, American Equity had agreed to this temporary arrangement. To which my reply was, 'Bullshit!'

It was whilst I was unsuccessfully trying to drum up some form of protest from the cast that an elderly actor playing a small role as one of the shepherds rebuked me most strongly with, 'You are a guest in this company and the only one protesting. We consider ourselves lucky to be working and grateful to the Guild for employing us!' This angered me even more. I was probably only half his age and it was beyond my comprehension that anyone should feel this mental forelock-touching necessary in gratitude for employment! In fact after a lifetime as an actor I wonder if I have ever been sufficiently in love with my profession. I always vowed it would never give me up, I would be the one to take the initiative if I thought it necessary.

We opened at Newhaven, Connecticut to good reviews and 'House Full' business, which was to be the pattern for the eight-week tour and the New York run. In fact I believe we set a record for the longest-running Shakespeare play on Broadway. I wonder if it still stands? I also remember that on that first night in Newhaven, Michael gave the most peculiar director's note I've ever heard in my life. We were all waiting to make our entrance for the second act when he appeared, wreathed in smiles, saying, 'It's going wonderfully, now get on and off as quick as you can!' My press was good and there were two notices that gave me particular pleasure. The *Boston Record* said: 'Another deposed sissy in Touchstone. Bill Owen plays him for the manly wiseacre he is, rather than the uppity-voiced daffodil you usually see.'

And a notice in the *Pittsburgh Sun* read: 'Into Touchstone the clown Mr Bill Owen pumps vibrant life and perhaps even more wit than his creator might have thought possible.'

Our New York opening at the Cort Theater was '*the* night' of that Broadway season. Hollywood was represented by all the glamour and glitz one associates with such an occasion. It was after an excellent reception, the flowers, the kissing and the congratulations that the final curtain fell, and as I hurried to my dressing room a voice enquired of me, 'Where is Kate's dressing room?' I turned, it was Cary Grant. Backstage was suddenly alive with these familiar faces, people I had known only from my seat at the local Odeon, and here they were, like Kate, for real. Robert Ryan, Ginger Rogers, Van Heflin and Uncle Tom Cobley an' all!

But after the celebration came the reality of settling down to what was obviously going to be a long run, and not helped by having to return nightly to my broom cupboard at the Wellington, marooned in that bedlam of a city. Relief came, however, in the form of a large bottle of Jack Daniel's and a letter with belated good wishes from Unity Theatre. The presence of the whisky was never explained, but the letter contained a postscript asking me to explore the possibility of obtaining the British rights for a production of *The Cradle Will Rock,* by Marc Blitzstein, which they wanted me to direct when I returned. By now I had found a friend in the company, the senior and much respected Irish actor, Whitford Kane; a veritable sage of the New York theatre scene he had been an original member of Orson Welles's Mercury Players, hence the title of the film *Citizen Kane.* Another boast of Whitford's was that he had played in the first production of *Strife* by John Galsworthy, in Liverpool.

So, naturally, it was to him that I went seeking advice and help. He knew Marc Blitzstein and, of course, Orson Welles, who had directed the play. He then took me for my first and only lunch at the Algonquin, the thespian refuge I couldn't afford. Over the meal he told me the extraordinary tale of *The Cradle Will Rock*. Described as a 'music drama' it told the story of a steel baron and his ugly fight against unionization. It was funded by the Federal Theater who, suddenly, within two days of the opening, withdrew the production and, to underline their determination, padlocked the Maxine Elliot Theater where the show was scheduled. Their reason was given as 'impending budget cuts' and the reshuffling of the Works Progress Administration, which meant, apparently, that no Federal Theater shows were to be opened until the start of the government's next fiscal year. Which was Washington's way, through pressure from conservative congressmen, of forestalling the opening of *Cradle* without seeming to have censored it. But they had not reckoned with Mr Welles who, within forty-eight hours, had raised the money for a lease on the Old Venice Theater uptown and who, in order to retain the scenery, had kept the truck driving around the city all day until the lease was signed.

It was rather ironic, however, that this show, the subject of which was 'union bashing', was also confronted at the last moment with what seemed insurmountable union problems, when both Actors' Equity and the Musicians' Union banned their members from appearing either on the stage or in the orchestra pit. They too failed to reckon with the ingenuity of the young Orson who put his actors among the audience where they simply said their lines and sang their songs, accompanied by the composer now seated at an upright piano on the stage, whilst he sat in the orchestra pit, narrating the story of what would have happened if only things had been normal – but union regulations had to be complied with! Despite these circumstances, it was an immediate success and both unions eventually relented and the show returned to normal.

Marc Blitzstein welcomed me as if I were an old friend, someone he'd known for years, which made evident the fact that Whitford had managed an excellent public relations job regarding Unity Theatre and my importance to its activities. The room he took me into gave more than an illusion of being cramped. A baby grand piano was piled high with books, magazines and musical scores, empty wine bottles lined the floor and an excess of furniture of dubious and ancient lineage overflowed the remainder of the room. In fact, as I recall, the only item clearly visible was a heavily burdened drinks trolley from which, having managed to seat me, Marc poured a very large Jack Daniel's the like of which I was not used to at eleven o'clock in the morning. Marc then sat at the piano, proclaiming he was about to play 'Ballad of the Easy Life' from *The Threepenny Opera* and would appreciate my opinion of his English translation. He then launched himself into song, but at such a pitch of decibels that I'd have been better sitting in the next room or even out in the street!

Now, whilst I will admit to my writing experience being almost exclusively employed for Unity Theatre – and therefore not confined to the inevitable subject of love, but also embracing the broader social and political issues – I had always worked within the idiom of the popular song. So, musically, what I was experiencing held no problems for me. Moreover, as a professional dance band vocalist I had sung my way through the best of Johnny Mercer, Frank Loesser and Sammy Cahn, to mention but a few. But I had been so excited about this day, and Whitford's story about Orson Welles and the show's beginnings had fired my enthusiasm. Accordingly I had arrived in Greenwich Village at least a half-hour too early and sat drinking coffee in a local diner, hardly able to contain myself in anticipation of listening to the score of *The Cradle Will Rock*. But instead, here I was listening to the English translation of a lyric, from what language I had no idea, not that it would have made any difference, not in the least helped by the fact that it was part of an opera. Neither were the lyrics inspiring. Take the line, 'There's not a dog from here to Timbuktu' – it doesn't quite have the same sophisticated sparkle of 'Moon River'. As for the music, it was haywire, with none of the notes following the way I thought they should. But I wanted that production of *The Cradle*. So my verdict was, of course: 'Superb ... Wonderful ... Couldn't be bettered', which was a big mistake because I'd let myself in for having to listen to the rest of the score. We eventually got around to the purpose of my visit and, thankfully, Marc's announcement that he didn't, after all, have time to play the rest as he had a lunch date with Kurt Weill (the composer of *The Threepenny Opera*). 'But, of course,' he said, 'you can do the show,' adding that he would inform his London agent, through whom we should make all the necessary arrangements.

I phoned Mick Manning as soon as I got back to my hotel. He was very excited but I was somewhat deflated, not to say drunk, after all my pent-up anticipation and so went to bed for the afternoon.

Later, after the show, I burst into Whitford's dressing room to give him the good news about *The Cradle*, only to be told by a friend of his waiting there that 'He's in the john.' He went on to say that he had seen the show and we talked about the production. I gathered he would have liked to have seen something more adventurous, which was when he congratulated me on my performance, adding these words, which will remain with me until the end, 'Of course, you are a dancer.' This, coming from Gene Kelly, had to mean something. He, one of the few greats, said that of me and I didn't even have a witness – Whitford was still in the 'john'!

With no show, Sunday could be a gloomy day, but there was always a little help from my company of friends with an occasional invitation to dinner or some other simple social event. With Whitford, it was usually a 'busman's holiday', such as a visit to the theatre, particularly on the fringe where one could find Sunday performances. It was at such a venue, housed within the Czech Institute, that we saw *Longitude 49*, an excellent play by Herb Tank, the leading role played by an unknown actor by the name of Sydney Poitier.

I particularly remember our visit to see this play because I read in the paper next day that some hoodlums had broken into the theatre during the night and wrecked the place, causing the show to be cancelled. What could possibly be gained by such vandalism? *Longitude 49* was a well-written, and I believe truthful, story of merchant seamen on the high seas; telling of their work, living conditions, economics, the aggravation of the ritual of class structure between officers and seamen and the inevitable clash of personalities caused by or exacerbated by long and cramped confinement. 'Truth in America is coming under suspicion,' was Whitford's rather poetic observation. He then told me of the rumblings of the House of Un-American Activities Committee, notorious for carrying out Senator McCarthy's increasingly hysterical anti-communist witch-hunts, which was to become a 'democratic' nightmare, involving persecution for some and for others the fear, then the shame of naming names. All so aptly described by Lillian Helman in *Scoundrel Time*, the book recounting her own experiences.

The William Morris Agency, one of the most influential in America, who now represented Myron Selznick in Britain, were taking care of me and during one of my rare visits to the office, I dropped the hint that any ideas they might come up with to boost my coffers would be more than welcome. Ideas they certainly had and within a couple of weeks I was booked for three plays on *Theater Guild of the Air*, a radio drama programme that went out every Sunday evening. I can only recall one and that was mainly because it starred Mickey Rooney in *National Velvet*. An objectionable young man, but what a talent! One day we found ourselves alone in the rehearsal room. What the circumstances were, I don't remember, but alone we were, and as he'd so far ignored me, I was somewhat surprised when he suddenly smiled, so I smiled back and returned to my newspaper. He began to hover, so I looked up, waiting for him to say something, but he didn't. Then he ambled over to a drum set in a corner and began to play. Now, I was a dance band drummer in my youth, no Gene Krupa, I'll admit, but I know good playing when I hear it, and what I heard was brilliant. It was the same when he moved to the piano; a momentary display of rare talent, crystal clear. I applauded and he gave a little mock bow before leaving the room. Had this been an attempt at communication? Whatever, he continued to ignore me to the end of the broadcast. Later I spoke with the producer, who was patiently suffering Mickey's tantrums. He said, 'Sam Goldwyn has to answer for him and Judy Garland, they'd both lived a life before they were out of their teens, there was nothing new!' I saw Mickey at the Savoy Theatre a couple of years ago in a show called *Burlesque*; he was still brilliant.

Although the contract I had signed was for the run of the play, it was understood in good faith that I would be away for no longer than five months – this had been promised by Michael Benthall at our first meeting. Yet here I was after seven months still playing in the biggest hit on Broadway.

But I was missing my family, particularly Edith, and celibacy didn't come easy. Such was my nature at the time that I had to be in love, surrounded by those who loved me. The total monotony of my room and life on a tight budget in New York City was the surest way of becoming an introvert – even for hardened New Yorkers. So began a kind of monastic existence, never leaving the hotel other than to eat in some cheap diner, killing the hours until it was time to head for the theatre. And even backstage, among the few friends I had, I began to make excuses to avoid any social invitations, under the delusion that my melancholy was apparent to no one but myself.

There was a temporary respite, however, and a return to normality when Edith phoned to say she could not stand our separation any longer. She had, she said, with Zan at boarding school made arrangements to park Tommy and a nanny with her parents in Scotland. She would be with me within a week!

I don't know how long we clung to one another when I met her at the airport. And even when our irate taxi driver came to look for us, I was too happy to mix words with him. I had taken an apartment for a week up on Central Park and it was like being on honeymoon – the one we never had. Edith saw the show as a guest of the management, after which we had a candlelight supper at the Plaza. It was during the meal that the thought crossed my mind, how could I possibly cope again without her? Almost in a panic I suggested I just walk out of the show and fly back with her! She laughed, thinking I was joking. I wasn't.

Then, as suddenly as she'd appeared, she'd gone. Everything seemed dark again. That was until a miracle happened a week or so later. A letter arrived from Anthony Darnborough, a producer with Rank, informing me that my presence was needed for a film and I should return as soon as possible. I almost flew round to the William Morris office where the wheels were set in motion.

Before I went home, however, they suggested I pay a brief visit to Hollywood, as their guest, 'to meet a few important people'. I politely declined; there was nowhere I wanted to go but home – preferably by boat. My American agents certainly were the 'Mr Fixits' of showbiz, one phone call and I was booked on the *Queen Mary*.

It was too good to be true – I was informed by the management that it was their intention to close the show in six weeks. I had already tendered my obligatory fortnight's notice, so what had this to do with me? They explained that Kate had refused to play with an understudy for longer than two weeks, which meant that after I left, in two weeks' time, the show would have to close early. Whilst this might sound like a back-handed compliment, the reality was that this company of actors who began as complete strangers and had become such good friends, would now lose four weeks' work! So I stayed for another two weeks, which seemed like two years. I lost my berth on the *Queen Mary* and had to go home on a damned aeroplane after all. Still, I must say it was far superior to the 'crate' that had brought me over. It was a Stratocruiser with more room, much comfort, service and a bar down below.

As I sat waiting for take-off, my mind wandered back over the past nine months and I asked myself, had anything been achieved? Then I thought of Whitford, my fellow actors, Bradford, PA and, of course, my wonderful Kate – and decided to put it all down to experience, but not to be repeated for a long, long time. My thoughts were interrupted by a latecomer being hustled to his seat, who, from a fleeting glance, I thought I recognized. Then I did something I've never done on an aeroplane since – I fell asleep.

The stewardess awakened me as we touched down at Goose Bay. It was then I saw the latecomer again as he passed along the gangway, and I knew I had to introduce myself. He had almost reached the Reception Hut when I caught up with him. 'My name is Bill Owen,' I said. 'I'm from Unity Theatre, Mr Robeson!' The moment I mentioned Unity Theatre, Paul's face lit up and very soon we were back on the plane, sitting in the little bar.

His playing at Unity had obviously left a great impression and I sat answering endless questions. I gathered he was on a visit to London to speak at some Congress or other. Things back in the States had not been easy for him of late. I had read a vilifying attack against him in the *New York Journal American*, a Hearst newspaper, alongside of which was an article hailing Senator McCarthy for having 'named' two 'pro-communist' State Department employees.

There was evidently a division of opinion among the left themselves as to exactly what Paul's political role should be, or whether he should even have a political role. Some argued that it would be better if he confined himself to singing for the cause of racial equality in America.

When he returned after this trip the pressures really began. Attempts to restrict his travel were finally successful. He was banned entirely from the National Broadcasting Corporation, which started with the cancellation of a show in which he was to appear as a guest of Eleanor Roosevelt. Paul Robeson was a man of such overwhelming talent that some considered it greater than his cause. This he denied and surely demonstrated as much throughout his life.

6

Delusions of Grandeur

I took my time getting used to being a family man once again, enjoying my son, for instance, a bundle of joy scuttling around the house on his bum with such speed and unerring sense of direction – but hardly to be recommended after the age of eighteen months! Then there was Edith. She and I had so many things to catch up on, some with more priority than others. So I took my time. But the fact could no longer be ignored that after three weeks I had still heard nothing about the forthcoming film which had been the cause of my hurried return home. I rang my agent who had heard nothing about it at all! 'I didn't even know you were home,' he cried. 'Why doesn't someone tell me what's going on?' To save any further hysterics, I promised to ring him back – what *was* going on? The answer came from an unexpected source when Edith admitted to a mild deception. Staying with me in New York, she had become increasingly concerned at the obvious stress I was living under. And this had been brought to a head when, over supper at the Plaza, I told her I could easily leave the play and return to England with her. 'And I would have taken you,' she said later. 'You were like a ghost of the man I'd married.' When she got home she immediately rang Anthony Darnborough, who as well as being a producer with the Rank Studios was an acquaintance of ours. Explaining her concern, she asked him to write to the New York Theater Guild requesting my return as there was a film for which I was needed. This he did, and home I came. I don't think I have ever loved any woman as much as I loved Edith as she made her 'confession'.

Unity Theatre threw a 'welcome home' shindig. Everyone was there, everyone I had worked with, argued with, and felt so at home with. We sang, danced and drank. In the midst of it all, Mick Manning, probably the best General Secretary Unity Theatre ever had, and I laid the foundation for my idea of doing a show based on the history of the British Music Hall – more of which later.

I must admit to no surprise when my agent informed me that the option on my contract would not be taken up by the Rank Organization. Why should they? The only film in which I had starred was *When the Bough Breaks*. I had also featured in *Easy Money*, *Trottie True* and *Once a Jolly Swagman*, but they never knew what to do with me and no one really had the time or inclination to find out. I suppose I should have simply acknowledged the fact that the party was over. When I became a contract player to J Arthur Rank he owned one hundred and forty of us, when I left there were fewer than twenty. I have to confess that I was not so much concerned with any 'artistic' failure as the grim reality, almost panic, at the fact that the regular, work-or-not pay-cheques had ceased.

Oddly enough at about that time pre-publicity notices began to appear in the trade press wrongly crediting to me films I hadn't actually appeared in! *Double Pursuit* was one, and *Highly Dangerous* another, the latter mentioned in a Bristol newspaper, saying something of what I was up to at the time:

> Bill Owen suffers the worst fate of his film career as Alf, Margaret Lockwood's friend in *Highly Dangerous*. He is murdered by a gang of European thugs and his body is dumped in Margaret Lockwood's bedroom.

Now, I ask you, who wouldn't remember being in her bedroom, dead or alive?

Following a visit from Edith's parents – 'To see your wee house,' as old Tom put it, but I was sure he was making certain I was doing right by his daughter – I was not surprised to receive a letter from him suggesting the house might be too small for us. Why, he asked, shouldn't we have the pleasure of a bigger and nicer one with him paying the difference as, he concluded, 'a late wedding present'.

I failed to see the logic in this. We had three bedrooms, they were small, but then the house was small and that's where we were living – I had a mortgage to prove it.

Edith, who had never gone along with my suspicions of her father's motives, was all for accepting his generous offer. I, on the other hand, was adamant that we should refuse it. She accused me of working-class snobbery and she was right. I had no logical explanation for my attitude then or now. Old Tom was offering to buy us a house as a wedding present in spite of my suspicions and ravings of 'Who's running our family, us or your father!' But the bare facts were that a larger house would be better for the children and I wouldn't be encumbered with a mortgage. Sanity prevailed, I pocketed my 'working-class snobbery' and we moved to Highgate. But there were still doubts, lingering doubts that I would perhaps never be able to provide a suitable life-style for Tom Stevenson's daughter. And wasn't it my mother who had said, 'You married out of your class, Billy.' It's a thought.

So, having no interest in gardening or pottering in the shed, keeping fit, becoming a Mason or even pursuing serious infidelity at that time, I went back to Unity and began research for the show I mentioned earlier, a history of the Music Hall. This took me to the British Museum library where for three weeks I found peace and contentment, a refuge I recommend to anyone who wants to 'get away from it all'.

This was my first experience of serious research and whilst I had no idea where to begin, I was determined it wasn't going to be just another 'Old Tyme Music Hall' with the usual ballads by Florrie Ford, Gus Elen, *et al*. The Music Hall was solely for the entertainment of the working class and whilst m'lords and ladies had their exclusive supper rooms, enjoying the gentility of oversweet Victorian songs, Music Hall produced its own entertainers from within its own audience. I grew up with variety theatre, the giant Moss Empire circuit that had a theatre in every city and large town throughout the country reigning supreme until it took ill through the popularity of the cinema and finally died with the advent of television.

Coincidentally, it was during my research, with the phone silent and the bills to be paid, but still having 'a name' from the few films I had made, that I was offered a few variety dates in the mid-fifties which included one or two on the Moss Empire circuit. So I dusted off my old cabaret act – 'You too can have a body like mine' – recruited Clive Dunn to join me as my 'assistant', and whilst I couldn't claim us a resounding success, we were always paid at the end of the week. It was on one of these dates at Torquay when Clive wasn't available and I played solo that I met up with the then little known double act of Morecambe and Wise. One day we were discussing the elusive lucky break that brings fame and fortune, something they were convinced would happen to them. Their philosophy was that when it was 'their turn' it would inevitably come. Ronnie Barker has said that talent will out – if you have it, it will surface. I'm nowhere near as sure. I have worked with many good actors whose turn never came to prove their talent. No, I go along with the adage of 'being in the right place at the right time for the right part'.

Meanwhile, back at the British Museum, I found that it was around the middle of the nineteenth century that 'Harmonic Evenings', held in a few inner London taverns with musical entertainment given by the reg'lars or local talent, had become extremely popular. It was Charles Morton, the licensee of the Canterbury Arms in Pimlico, who had the idea of building a large room, attached to his tavern, to accommodate an ever-growing audience. In fact, the room became a hall big enough to hold over one thousand people, thereby heralding the Music

Hall. I also discovered the score and libretto of a short entertainment described as a *burletta*, of which the *Oxford Companion of Music* says: 'In 18th-century Britain the word was applied to a light type of musical entertainment, something of the type of Ballad Opera.'

I also deduced that it was probably the songs from such mock operas that eventually became part of the musical repertory of the Supper Rooms. So here was an opportunity to show the upper and lower orders at play, with m'lords stirred by ballads of heroism and battlefields, of love, tenderness and Victorian virginity, whilst the lower orders, no doubt ignorant of such behaviour, were more forthright in their emotional expressions, getting to grips with such favourites as 'As Soon as I Touched me Seaweed, I Knew it was Going to be Fine', or the social comment of 'The 'Ouses in Between'.

So the Unity show began with a Burletta followed by an Harmonic Evening in the Canterbury Arms. The second part was devoted entirely to the Music Hall where chaos reigned for several minutes as the stage was invaded by suffragettes. With the perfect title, *Winkles and Champagne*, from the book by Wilson Disher and directed by yours truly, it was to prove another triumph for Unity Theatre. It remained in the repertory in various guises until the theatre's destruction by fire in November 1975.

All this talk of Music Hall has reminded me of my dear friend Leonard Sachs whose obituary revived happy memories of our work together at the Players Theatre. My début was in 1944 when it was temporarily housed in a large basement in Mayfair before transferring to a converted railway arch in Villiers Street, Charing Cross. Leonard's national popularity came, of course, with his role as Chairman in the much loved TV show, *The Good Old Days*. The best thing I can say about the wages at the Players is that they helped to keep the wolf out of the bed! But one was always in good company with the likes of Peter Ustinov, Bernard Miles, Patricia Hayes and Hattie Jacques, to mention but a few. Without doubt Leonard was the most brilliant director the Players ever had. And nothing exemplifies this more than his staging of the duet 'Tell Me Pretty Maiden' for Hattie and myself. The scene shows her on a swing, all red bloomers and petticoats. Then I appear as a short-arsed Guardsman, pill-box hat, scarlet tunic and trousers far too long, collapsing into more wrinkles than you-know-who's stockings!

I also carried, or dragged, a long sword, in its scabbard of course, but which nevertheless proved to be of some embarrassment to Miss Jacques during the course of our dance! It was a riot, and they offered to put us on the bill at the London Palladium, but Hattie declined. She was probably right, the piece had been created for the intimacy of the Players.

In 1951 came the Festival of Britain, a kind of self-congratulatory 'knees-up', after having picked ourselves off the floor. After all the suffering and shortages, we were now looking forward to the future for ourselves and our children. Proper health care, full employment with no exploitation, better education for all and dignity with old age. By God, we were going to get it right this time!

With such beliefs, dreams, excitement and pageantry throughout the land there was no place for the cynic, particularly in London. Wherever one went it was just one huge celebration, part of which was the Festival Gardens in Battersea Park. Vaguely modelled on the nineteenth-century pleasure grounds, Vauxhall Gardens, there were avenues of trees illuminated by coloured lights, the whole area resounding to music, dancing and all the fun of the fair, and there was a theatre, too.

The theatre was built especially for the Festival and resembled a pink-and-white iced birthday cake. As for the show *The Festival Song Saloon*, let me refer you to the *Tatler* of 25 July 1951, which had this to say:

... An hour before this enchanting little world-in-itself [the Festival Gardens] is plunged into darkness, Mr Leonard Sachs opens his Song Saloon. It is his business to induce in us the illusion that we are traditional Londoners on the spree, gay, raffish and uninhibited. Mr Sachs is the very man for the job. The root of the tradition is in him. With Peter Ridgeway he started the 'Latejoys' in 1936. Their first theatre was at the King Street corner of Covent Garden in the building originally occupied by Evans Song and Supper Rooms, to which Thackeray often went in search of conviviality and characters and are now to be found under the arches in Villiers Street.

Of the turns that Mr Sachs presents, most have a chorus and all of them are redolent of a time when people went to the music-hall in virile, boisterous mood and every performance had a Bank Holiday ring to it. Miss Daphne Anderson is the elegant lady in enduring corset trouble. Mr Philip Godfrey, the garrotter, who, fixing us with one baleful eye from the steps of the scaffold, damns us all; Miss Patricia Hayes, the pathetic child who pleads with us to sell no more drink to her father; Mr Bill Owen, the athlete, too enfeebled to stand up to the strain of his own enthusiasm for health and beauty, and Mr Edric Connor, a coloured singer of 'Lily of Laguna'. Mr Sachs has also his Sylphides (Mlles Maria Sanina, Eve Wakefield and Lulu Dukes), who wear his ecstatic praises to the manner born. In sum, the show has a flavour, just the flavour needed to complete the evening's pleasure.

In 1952 Kitty Black, Director of the Company of Four, sent me a play called *The Square Ring*, a story set among boxers and their handlers during an evening of contests held in a dingy stadium. Through the dressing room parades a group of 'hope-to-bes', 'maybes' and 'has-beens' who point out the moral that the noble art is a tough, rough and corrupt game at best and only a few have the sense to call a halt. It was

suggested that I play the part of the 'handler', the man who
tends to the boxers' needs for the fight, and their bruises and
blood when they've finished, but I chose to play the joker in
the pack, 'Happy Coombs'. When Kitty pointed out that it
wasn't a leading role, I replied, 'True, but it's the only one
with any hope.'

We opened at the Lyric Theatre, Hammersmith, and at the
dress rehearsal when I entered in boxing gear, Kitty was heard
to scream from the stalls, 'But he looks like a boxer!' What
did she expect me to look like – Les Dawson? But wait, read
the critic from *Punch* (very apt):

> This midget Cockney dynamo is given tremendous verve by
> Mr Bill Owen. If you can imagine Mr Fred Astaire born in
> Brixton you will have an idea, not only of Mr Owen's spry
> excellence, but also how he looks.

We had rave notices and consequently the management of the
Company of Four sent us out on tour whilst they sought a
West End theatre. The notices on tour were even better than
London, but the business wasn't. Nobody came, we played to
'washers'. I remember a foggy matinée at the Opera House,
Manchester, a barn of a place, where it was impossible to see
whether there was anyone in the theatre or not. That was
until I made my entrance, when I took off my camel-hair
overcoat and threw it to the handler with the line, 'Take care
of that, it's paid for!' That always brought a big laugh, but in
that fog-filled auditorium all we heard in the distance from
the back of the stalls was a little, chortled, 'Haw-haw!' which
brought on a nasty coughing spasm, and that was the only
sign of life we had all afternoon.

While I was on tour with this play a most extraordinary
occurrence took place on stage. It was during an altercation
between Happy Coombs and a crooked boxing manager,
played by John Colicos, a Canadian actor who, in mid-scene,
suddenly dropped the mask of his character and threatened
me personally with physical violence after the show. I can't

remember the actual words he used, I was so dumbfounded. When I spoke to the company manager who had witnessed the scene, he admitted to nothing more than, 'I think Colicos came on a bit strong with the language during the scene,' but dismissed any idea of it being personal. But I knew the man wasn't acting, he had lost control, the anger, the hatred, the threat were real. But why? Socially our paths had never crossed during the entire run of the play. The only time we met was on stage, in character, so how could it be anything personal? Was this another 'Hughie'? Was it once again because of the success of the character? Everything I felt about Happy Coombs had come to pass. Whilst the play may have been 'a well-informed document about this brutal sport', the only ray of hope was Happy, he was the clown amidst the gloom. He stole the play, as I knew he would.

It was many years later, when I was playing with Spike Milligan and the beautiful Joan Greenwood in *Son of Oblomov* at the Comedy Theatre, that one night, as Joan and I waited backstage to take the curtain call, I related the Colicos incident to her. She showed little surprise and told me the story of how, during the rehearsal of a play with the Old Vic Company, of which both her husband André Morell and John Colicos were members, Colicos for no apparent reason struck André, knocking him off a rostrum. 'The man's a maniac,' she concluded. By the way, despite his threat, nothing happened. But I should add that the late Bill Travers, a pal of mine in the show, insisted on walking me back to my digs that night – he was a big man, even in his socks!

Another reminder of that ill-fated tour was playing Nottingham when I struck 'Rottweiler' digs again. My heart sank as the taxi pulled up outside 'Prompt Corner', two terraced, back-to-back cottages containing, as I was soon to discover, a maze of gas-lit passages, just like something from Dickens. My hostess, a Mrs Gregory, whose walk I once heard likened to that of a saddle-sore parrot, ran a 'tight ship' and divided her guests into two categories: manual workers, mainly builders' labourers, who occupied one cottage, and non-manual workers such as poor actors and barrel-bellied, shiny-blue-suited types who called themselves commercial travellers in the other. The bathroom floor was covered with odd pieces of sodden lino which gurgled when trodden on. The giant iron bath which sometime in the last century had been painted yellow had now been scrubbed to a battleship grey and almost dominated the cathedral-like proportions of the room. On a far wall of the bathroom was a second door, locked and without a clue as to where it led. I settled into a looked-forward-to wallow in barely five inches of lukewarm water and not a bit of soap in sight. I was pondering the thought that at the very moment my wife and children were most likely enjoying their breakfasts in our lovely Highgate home when there came a loud pounding on the mystery door. It grew louder and louder and what followed went something like this:

ME	What do you want?
VOICE OFF 1	Excuse me, surr, would ye moind openin' the door?
ME	What the hell for?
VOICE OFF 1	Well, you see, surr, we've been lookin' for the doinin' room.
ME	I'm having a bath!
VOICE OFF 2	We've lost our way, surr!
ME	What's the bathroom got to do with it?
VOICE OFF 3	Can ye get to the doinin' room through there?
ME	Yes, but...
VOICE OFF 2	If ye wouldn't moind, we've been lookin' for half an hour.
VOICE OFF 3	Found ourselves out in the street twoice!
VOICE OFF 1	We'd be most obliged, surr.

So I got out of the bath, skidded my way across the sodden lino, and, finding the key hanging above it, unlocked the door. Immediately I was confronted by three large, robust Irishmen in their best Sunday blue off-to-Mass-followed-by-the-pub

suits. They trooped past me, fingers to forelocks as I held the
door open for them. The last one, and the tallest, looked down
at my nakedness and I swear he chuckled!

The Square Ring folded on the road and we all went home
to do our own thing which meant waiting for the phone to
ring. Fortunately, I didn't have to wait long. I very soon found
myself rehearsing in a new play by Ted Willis, *The Magnificent
Moodies*, which opened at the Embassy Theatre, Swiss
Cottage. It lasted three weeks and was never heard of again.
What it was about, I haven't a clue, but there were rumours
about it being a comedy! Then, much to my surprise, came a
sudden burst of film activity with *Hotel Sahara* starring Yvonne
de Carlo, David Tomlinson, Peter Ustinov and, among others,
me. There was *The Story of Robin Hood*, a Walt Disney
production in which Richard Todd played Robin, and I played
Will Stutely alongside an unknown from Australia enjoying
himself as the Sheriff of Nottingham – one Peter Finch. James
Hayter played Friar Tuck.

But the point of this catalogue of activity is to explain a
unique occurrence – which was that I now had a credit balance
at the bank, which in those days was doubly creditable! It
went to my head. I announced to Edith we should move to
the country, perhaps near Pinewood where we would be among
the 'élite'.

We could even join the 'merry-go-round' – which I'd been
so much against not long before – and the air would be good
for the children. Edith objected, the house we had was more
than adequate, it was delightful and moreover it was paid for.
Of course, if I had been honest I would have admitted to her
that the whole crazy idea was simply me trying to prove to
her that I was capable of making decisions for my own family.
But I was adamant, we moved to the country. From where we
were in London, a trip on the underground would have taken
us into the countryside, but not to Lavender Lodge down by
the river at Maidenhead. I bought it, with a heavy mortgage,
from a member of the Poupart family, the famous jam-

makers whose fortune, I'm sure, gave their life-style a certain consistency, which could hardly be said of my source of income. But there was no doubt the house was near Pinewood Studios. However, I have to admit that during our three or four years in residence I never had one call to appear in a film there!

There I was, the country gent, with half an acre, complete with a dog who regarded my command to heel with utter disdain. He hated the sight of me, but revelled in obeying and enjoying the rest of the family. He stood guard over little Tommy, defending him with his life, even from me! But I did receive the respect I was due from the staff. Oh, yes, I had staff – cook-housekeeper, char, part-time gardener, and nanny as and when required. I soon discovered, despite the accusations aimed at me of fascist tendencies as a director when I needed to get my own way, that when it came to giving orders to the domestics, it all became far too chummy. For example, the gardener...

'Mornin', Bill.'
'Mornin', Fred.'
'By the way, Bill, I shall need annuver free 'undred daffodil bulbs.'
'Right-ho, Fred, I'll give you a cheque.'
'I'd prefer cash, Bill.'

Fred was a 'refugee' from Essex, who ran a sort of mini-garden centre with his brother-in-law. You know the kind of thing – 'One for Bill, two for us.' Edith had no such difficulties, she carried her own authority, she was born to it. I was like putty in their hands. But it was a charming house, built on colonial lines, not grand, just enough room for Edith and me and the two children to spread ourselves. Never have I wanted something so much as Lavender Lodge to be a success.

I had never met Basil Dearden the film director who, out of the blue, called me on the phone, somewhat belatedly I thought, to congratulate me on my performance in *The Square Ring*. He told me that with his partner Michael Relph they had purchased the film rights of the play. My heart leapt! He was going to offer me Happy Coombs in the film! Why else would a director of his stature bother to phone me? He continued, 'Although we have never met, I felt I had to tell you personally that as much as I would like to, I cannot offer you your original role.' He then explained that a certain filmstar, now a venerable knight, was considering the role with the stipulation that should he accept, I would not play Happy Coombs. I felt like thanking him for nothing! Was I back again with the 'Hughie' problem?

In the event, however, the threat did not materialize. A couple of weeks later Dearden phoned again. 'He has turned down the script ... I want you to play Happy Coombs!'

7

Visions of Grandeur

So the preparation for the film began. A gym was erected in one of the studios at Ealing, with a boxing ring, punch bags and all the rest of the necessary boxing paraphernalia, where we would appear with our doubles for a morning's work-out. Only one enthusiastic young actor, Ronald Lewis, declined the aid of a double. Someone was heard to comment, 'He must be out of his tiny, bleedin' Chinese mind!' and everyone looked at me! Mind you, I can remember a session with my double when he did no more than give me a tap and I immediately fell down! To him it was a light blow – but his name was Dave Crowley, a Lonsdale Belt lightweight and very famous during his days of glory. He was my height and married to a very tall lady who, he complained, knocked him about. But he was a genuine cockney who always saw the bright side of life and we became great friends. The last I heard of him he was coaching lads in a London Boys Club. Robert Beatty played the lead in a strong company which included Bill Travers, Jack Warner, George Rose, Maxwell Reed and myself. The filming went like clockwork and the results were very rewarding for me. I was to play major roles in a further three films for Basil Dearden and Michael Relph.

I left one uncompleted venture at Unity, a theatre adaptation of Howard Spring's novel, *Fame is the Spur*. It was inspired after seeing the film version during my stay in New York.

Craig Timberlake, a member of the *As You Like It* company, had been with me; he also had one or two literary efforts to his credit, so we settled down to it together. I brought it home and handed it to Mick Manning who became very excited and duly submitted it to Howard Spring, asking his permission to present it.

We eventually received a curt reply from Howard Spring which read: 'The adaptation is more than adequate, but *Fame is the Spur* is not a political novel.'

Not political? Well, I don't know, Mr Howard Spring – you could have fooled me! I had always been under the impression that the main subject of this novel concerns the rise to power of one John Hamer Shawcross, a Labour politician. In reality it is the life story of the British Labour Prime Minister Ramsay McDonald.

My life as a country gent began well, coinciding with the offer in 1954 of a leading role in Basil Dearden's new film *The Rainbow Jacket*, a tale of the Sport of Kings involving a bent bookmaker and a banned jockey who still hangs around the race tracks. The jockey strikes up a father-figure relationship with a young lad who aspires to wear the colours, and when he does is prepared to pull the race to save him from the mob. The script, sympathetically and gently written, came from the pen of T B Clarke and it proved a very successful film. The young lad was played by an unknown, Fella Edmunds, who after his brief moment of glory seemed to disappear back into the unknown. My girlfriend was played by Kay Walsh. Other stalwarts included Sid James, Bernard Lee and Edward Underdown, while two Jockey Club stewards were played by Wilfrid Hyde White and Robert Morley who, both being regular punters, seemed to write their own script as they went along! Sir Gordon Richards made a guest appearance. Many years later Willie Carson, giving a TV interview, said it was seeing the film as a schoolboy that had made him determined to be a jockey. Like *The Square Ring*, *The Rainbow Jacket* was made at Ealing Studios under the flag of Sir Michael Balcon.

The preparations prior to the making of the film included working with an animal for which I have no particular love – the horse. The Acton Rowbothams, I'm the first to admit, do not come from an equestrian background. My learning experience was arduous, somewhat dangerous and downright painful. My first morning 'out' was taken under the watchful eye of Mr Smith of Holyport, an instructor with royal connections I was told. He had me jogging, bareback, around the paddock. Of course, I was totally unprepared for this and wore no protection whatsoever. Without going into details I am sure even the ladies will appreciate my predicament as matters almost came to the crunch! Then, damn me, only a few weeks later on location at Kempton, if another of these temperamental brutes didn't kick me in the same place. Edith happened to be with me that day so I at least didn't have to explain the bruises. But she did show some concern as I stood there clasping my breeches, enquiring of Sir Michael Balcon, 'He isn't damaged, is he?'

As I have already mentioned, it was during the making of the film that I learned of the death of my father, a loss which affected Edith almost as much as it did me. They had grown very close during our marriage. This I believe was due to his sympathy, understanding and affection for her, qualities that had been missing in the relationship she had with her own father. The emotions were there of course, but hidden. It was pitiful to watch the frustration of both as Edith and her father tried to communicate, but Old Tom could only find expression through material things. Another reason for my father's fondness for Edith was the grandson she had presented him with, whom he adored.

My father had been treated for a chest cold when in fact he was suffering from pneumonia. The panel doctor had given him a bottle of bright green medicine; I saw it on the shelf in the scullery on the day of the funeral. The colour, I suppose, was of as little significance as the medicine itself. He had been the Union Delegate for the Hanwell Trolley Bus Depot which may have given him sufficient importance to explain the presence of two officials from London Passenger Transport.

They, with great ceremony, presented my mother with a certificate and a cheque for fifty pounds. Was this then the sum total of his worth after a lifetime of labour and two wars? Dylan Thomas raged at the death of his father:

> Do not go gentle into that good night,
> Old age should burn and rave at close of day ...

Well, my dear father did all his burning and raving when he was alive, on behalf of his fellow man.

Once again I returned to the theatre, this time in the company of Mai Zetterling and Herbert Lom, to appear in a drama called *The Trap* which, the management assured us, had been a smash hit ... in Hungary! Now if that was kosher all I can say is something must have been lost in transit. It was a disastrous four-week tour with crucifying notices. For example, one Oxford critic closed his review by saying, 'At the end of the play Mr Lom goes to prison; I thought this was a very good idea.' We struck novel digs in Edinburgh – the place also served as a brothel! I wasn't particularly perturbed, but, oh boy, the rumpus at night! By this time, by the way, Mai Zetterling was referring to the play as *The Crap*. We opened hastily at the Duke of York's Theatre and the author travelled all the way from Hungary to see his masterpiece; he was just in time, we closed after three weeks.

The commercial theatre is always a gamble for all concerned, except for Andrew Lloyd Webber of course, whereas with film work the wages are usually assured. So back I went to the old routine and the phone stopped ringing again. But, now an aspiring country gent, I had to keep up appearances and that went through my bank balance like the proverbial dose of salts. I was in the right frame of mind, then, when my agent rang to tell me that Jack Payne, a popular pre-war band leader now treading the minefield of theatrical management, had offered me the tour of a play. My immediate response was yes, before making any further enquiries.

The play, a slight comedy by R F Delderfield entitled *Where There's a Will*, had been given a try-out at the Q Theatre near Richmond, but all to no avail. Leslie Dwyer who had played the lead in the production was not interested in the tour and the character – a cockney who inherits a share in a West Country farm which causes a certain amount of consternation – was now to be played by Eric Barker, a popular comedian. Was I interested in playing a subsidiary character with the name Fred Slater? 'I know nothing about the part,' my agent haughtily informed me. 'They haven't even bothered to send me a script.' They at least sent one to me. I pocketed my ego and once again said yes.

We opened in Nottingham and Mr Delderfield invited me to join him for supper after the first night of the show. Expecting a cast party I was somewhat surprised to find that his only other guests were his agent, the director and Jack Payne. Delderfield explained the point of the gathering, which was that he wanted to build up my part, make it more important by changing some of the situations. He was very enthusiastic and wanted to get down to rewriting that night. Whilst it had to be seen as a compliment, I had certain forebodings. Was this too going to become another 'Hughie' situation? In the play, Fred Slater is a spiv, a wartime hustler, a pedlar who came from under the counter, knowing the price of everything and the value of nothing. In the post-war years the comedian Sid Field had brought him to life as Slasher Green, a comic cartoon character. But I had known these types so well; I'd once lived among them! There was no doubt that with the alterations the play was funnier and did good business, so Jack Payne decided to bring it into town. Eric Barker, however, declined so Leslie Dwyer was approached about taking over his role again, and he agreed. But when we gathered for rehearsals at the Garrick Theatre, where we were to open, I discovered to my horror that Leslie had not been informed of the changes to the play whilst we were on tour. The director told me he intended to explain as he went along! How do you explain to an actor that in his absence his role – the hub of the play, the character around which it had revolved – was now to be replaced by a subsidiary character?

Naturally, the first day's rehearsal was embarrassing to say the least and I informed the director that if there was to be any repetition I would remove myself to the café next door, returning only after the whole situation had been explained to Leslie and rehearsals could continue undisturbed – or else!

The play opened to fair notices but the situation between Leslie and I was never really resolved – how could it be? The review in the *Sunday Times* certainly indicated that our roles had reversed:

> ... some highly professional playing, and some skilful amputation, have now inspirited a new vitality into the piece. The part of the brother-in-law, originally a subordinate role, has now, in the hands of Bill Owen, become the rock-certain peg upon which the rest of the comedy is hung.

Meanwhile, back at Lavender Lodge, the landed gentry scene, with *Country Life, House and Garden* and *Vogue*; etc. left casually on the coffee table, was really not for me. I had to face the fact that as a good jobbing actor I was never going to be able to keep a show like this on the road. Now, if I had been sensible and become a jam-maker, like the previous owners, who knows, Edith and I might have lived happily ever after.

As for the domestic staff, they had been reduced to a twice-weekly visit from the charlady. A lodger had been found to occupy the servants' quarters and entertaining had been whittled to a minimum. But on the odd occasion when we had to push the boat out, I found myself courting a hernia mowing the lawn. One of the unkindest cuts occurred when we had to give up our pre-dinner whiskys, substituting cheap

Spanish plonk. I remember getting drunk on it – once – something I would not advise. All this may sound melo-dramatic, but that's the way I saw it. Finally we had to say farewell to Lavender Lodge, with me standing on the lawn, which badly needed cutting, by the way, stoned out of my tiny mind in the wee small hours, waving a near-empty bottle of El Gut Rot, yelling insults at this gracious house. But, aristocrat that it was, it merely smiled back, aloof and contemptuous in the moonlight. Drunk as *I* was I knew what it was intimating: 'It was never going to work, you know.' Then Edith and little Tommy appeared, both in their night clothes, and led me back to bed.

By the time I was making *The Ship that Died of Shame* for Basil Dearden from the novel by Nicholas Monsarrat, we had moved to Brighton, an upheaval I missed as I was busy with Richard Attenborough and George Baker chasing up and down the English Channel in a motor torpedo boat. Having given up all pretensions to a country life, I vowed no house would ever own me again, but later I was to have the experience of being disowned by one. In the meantime, we started again in a large rambling Regency flat in Sussex Square. It had no airs or graces, it was just a comfortable home. I accept that places must change with time and the views of an octogenarian must be regarded with tolerance and sympathy. However, I do believe that Brighton has lost its character and the individuality that once made it the most unique seaside resort in the British Isles. It has picked up the bad manners and habits of London. It was a delight to live there during the fifties and sixties, retaining still the fading glimmer of the notorious thirties, the original images of its grandeur and history, the nooks and crannies, cobbled squares, shadowy passageways and little cottages that seemed to be hiding away. And people smiled. I became very attached to Brighton, I felt safe there and yet it was to prove a place of momentous changes in my life.

Brighton has always been a haven for showbiz folk – Lord Olivier and Max Miller were almost neighbours! Dora Bryan could be seen entertaining Lady Clements with an aperitif on her patio, Danny La Rue and his retinue might be seen at weekends taking the air along the front and waving to Dame Margot Fonteyn and her husband, Dr Roberto Arias, or Brenda de Banzie talking to Elizabeth Allen or Gilbert Harding.

Edith took to all of this like a duck to water. The hospitality became almost competitive, one's guests for a social occasion had to be booked well in advance, which meant sometimes on a Sunday you could meet the same guests twice, once at midday for lunchtime drinks and then at a dinner party somewhere in the evening, which usually meant most topics of conversation had already been exhausted. I quickly drew a line at those double events, it was just like a matinée day in the theatre.

The first time I met Oscar Lewenstein was with Ted Willis when they set up a professional company at Unity Theatre in the late 1940s, from which I absolved myself of any responsibility, because I didn't consider it to be a viable proposition. I was proved right. The second time Oscar and I met he had become a respected impresario who, with his company Peachum Productions, was about to present the British première of *The Threepenny Opera*, book and lyrics by Bertolt Brecht, music by Kurt Weill, and he was offering me the leading role in *Mack the Knife*.

What a role, what a gift of a role! Well, it certainly turned out to be under Sam Wanamaker's direction and one of the most exciting theatrical experiences of my life. I shall always remember the gathering for the first rehearsal, Georgia Browne, Daphne Anderson, Warren Mitchell and Eric Pohlman, to mention just a few of the large company. Then the MD played the songs to us and it brought back memories of New York, Greenwich Village, spring 1950 and Marc Blitzstein's flat where I first heard the score, six years before...

It was a part demanding total concentration during both

acting and singing and gave me probably the greatest entrance of my career.

The entire first scene is taken by the ballad singer (Ewan MacColl) who sings to the passing crowd of the exploits of Mack the Knife. 'Oh the shark has pretty teeth, dear ...'

Then I made my entrance in a single spotlight, top hat, white tie and tails, with a scarlet lined cloak. And I'll never forget Sam's instructions at rehearsal: 'You enter with the grace of a dancing Fred Astaire!'

And what a first night! The Royal Court Theatre was packed with everybody who was anybody in showbiz, including the usual dilettantes. During the interval, Claude Cockburn, the well-known Irish journalist, whom I'd never met before, found his way into my dressing room, spewed into the sink, congratulated me and left! After all the clamour Edith and I had a quiet supper with Kitty and Malcolm Muggeridge, staying the night with them at their flat in Albany, off Piccadilly. The next day, to celebrate my notice by Robert Wraight in the *Star* – 'A Brilliant Mack the Knife' – Edith bought me a new cap, still the same size, from Lock's in St James's. I normally bought mine from Dunns!

One evening as I sat in my dressing room waiting for my call, the phone rang. The caller, a woman, after establishing that she was talking to me, enquired in tones both dulcet and sensuous whether I would like to take her to bed. Now, call me naive, unworldly if you like, but I was a little surprised at this unconventional opening gambit from a complete stranger. I admit to hesitating, after all I was preoccupied with giving a performance of a very different nature, but my dresser arrived in time to say I was required on the stage. A couple of nights later the phone rang again. A different voice this time, very sophisticated, more Roedean than Romford, but the invitation was basically the same, 'Why don't we meet for a little fun?'

This one gave her name, 'Faith', which I thought was a touch ironical. I managed to ask her if she made a habit of

ringing strange men with such proposals. 'You're no stranger,'
she replied. 'I was in the audience this afternoon.' She then
proceeded to explain how I as this cheap Lothario who treated
women like whores had 'turned her on'. Perversely, she then
rang off. I'm still no wiser as to her identity and never received
another invitation. *The Threepenny Opera* was a great show
and later it transferred to the Comedy Theatre, but it didn't
run for long. It seems that the ever-faithful, middle-class,
theatre-going audiences were not yet ready to have their
conventions and lethargy disturbed. Perhaps it might have
been better to wait for the first rumblings from Sloane Square
where George Devine would turn the London theatre on its
head with *Look Back in Anger*, by an unknown playwright
named John Osborne.

Tommy was now at prep school and I missed him. He and I
have always been great friends, a relationship that began to
blossom the morning I arrived back from America. He was
about one year old. I have always felt an affinity between us –
as mates we enjoy each other's company. I can't ever recall
the need to lay down hard and fast rules. There was one
occasion when I caught him out in some half-truth and I
warned him that he must never tell me a lie again. Then, after
second thoughts, added, 'If you can avoid it.' Well, I reasoned,
even at the age of five he needs a little elbow room in which
to manoeuvre, bearing in mind the world he would have to
grow up in. To my knowledge he has never abused it.

I was, however, adamant that I would never buy him any
toy firearms, in fact anything to do with war. He had to
understand my utter loathing for war. To my surprise he
accepted the latter quite philosophically, but I have a suspicion
that he had long since come to the conclusion that he had a
bit of a nutter for a father. As regards the toy firearms, he
suggested a compromise. 'Can I borrow a gun from Timothy?'
(his best friend). I had to admit to a nagging conscience, after
all a total arms embargo seemed rather harsh. So I 'let battle

commence' and the 'wars' rang around Sussex Square as Germans fell and Cowboys and Indians bit the dust just as they had done when I was a boy; enemies were consistent and recognizable in those days. However, Tommy's explaining the reason to his friends for his lack of weaponry was to lead to my inadvertently declaring an armistice at the onset of hostilities. One morning, Tommy having been re-armed by his friend, the Square reverberated with the noise of battle, proving just how much of a racket a dozen or so boys can make – until I appeared. Immediately there was a deafening silence and they all stood as still and as silent as statues. My embarrassment was added to when neighbours unused to this sudden lull – any lull – came to their windows. Edith came to the front door just in time to see me picking my way through these stationary little figures, every one armed to the teeth, on my way to the bus stop around the corner.

And now he was already going away to school. His visits every third weekend were not enough for me. Ours was a special relationship, very similar to the one I had enjoyed with my father. His name was already down for Lancing College, the fees to be paid from his grandfather's will. Well, why not? As far as Edith was concerned this was the normal course to be followed. But to me it meant, not only conflict with my principles, but also that he and I would miss the everyday companionship, the sharing of his formative years. Most of his time would be spent with strangers and I resented it. But gradually, in spite of my preaching to Edith my long-held belief of equal rights for all (a doctrine she had paid lip-service to, agreeing out of her love for me) I seemed to be undergoing a kind of metamorphosis, reluctantly acceding to her preconceived notions of what our life-style should be. I can even remember hearing myself say at one of our cocktail parties, 'We've got Tommy down for Lancing, you know.' I think I was, for the first and last time, trying to rid myself of 'the chains that bind', my socialist ideals. Don't misunderstand me, there's nothing wrong with that if one is honest and convinced.

I was neither and began to lose my own identity.

Adding to my sense of domestic desolation was the fact that work was becoming spasmodic, the periods of telephone silence were getting longer. It was during one of these lulls of inactivity that I decided to try and write a commercial play. With my experience of writing for Unity Theatre this was to be the first time I had seriously contemplated trying it for 'bread'.

Breakout was the story of an unmarried woman who is held captive in her home for twenty-four hours by an escaped convict and the developing relationship that builds up between them. Whatever I may have felt about it, which wasn't a great deal, my opinion wasn't shared by the lady who was typing the script. She rang to say how much she had enjoyed the play and as she was a kind of 'scout' for a Dutch impresario and literary agent, would I mind if she showed it to him? Of course, I agreed and a week later I had a phone call from the gentleman concerned, Hans Keuls. We made a date to meet over lunch when he suggested minor alterations to which I agreed. Once made, a script was sent to Amsterdam, contracts were signed and I duly received a cheque for one hundred pounds for a year's option. This had happened in less than a month of my handing in the original script to be typed.

I attended the world première of *Breakout* in Rotterdam, understanding very little other than that interpreted by my theatrical agent, Felix de Wolfe, who is of Dutch extraction.

Whilst there I learned that the theatre was rebuilt using the bricks from the old building, destroyed by German bombing and that it was one of the first to rise from the ruins. The play was eventually presented at the Belgrade Theatre in Coventry, coincidentally the first new theatre to rise from the ruins in this country. I directed and played the lead opposite one of my favourite ladies, Cherry Morris.

It was through my work with the Royal Court that I met lighting director Andrew Philips, who introduced me to a company of actors in Brighton known as Group 1, for whom he asked me to write a play. I wrote *Fringe of Light*, for their début at the Edinburgh Festival Fringe. There was marvellous and unexpected publicity prior to the opening due to two plain-clothes policemen turning up at a rehearsal, demanding a copy of the script but giving no reasons. The next morning it hit the fan: 'Police Investigate Fringe Play'. What publicity! – and free, too. The police refused to comment. More headlines! What it was all about I don't know, unless it was the complaint made by the local Roman Catholic Church whose hall had been hired for the presentation. The script was duly returned the next day and the play opened – it was a disaster!

Matters improved, however. I had a telephone call from Peter Rogers, brother-in-law of Sydney Box, the man who'd had sufficient faith in me to put me under contract with Rank. It was Peter who had written the screenplay for *When the Bough Breaks*, the first film I starred in. Now, some ten years later, he wanted to know if I would like to be in a film he was producing called *Carry On Sergeant*.

I was told it was adapted from either a play or a novel, but if the film script was anything to go by it was not only based on a very unlikely premise but bolstered by every known army gag and comedy situation since Kitchener. However, when I saw the cast list which included Dora Bryan, Bob Monkhouse, Ken Connor, Charles Hawtrey and Eric Barker, I knew the comedy was in safe hands. I played the corporal and the sergeant was played by William Hartnell who I thought never quite captured the mood of the piece. When asked what I thought the chances of the film were, I admitted to some doubt. My reasoning was that by the late fifties the British cinema-going public were watching high-quality, sophisticated movies such as *Room at the Top*, *The Old Man and the Sea*, and *Cat on a Hot Tin Roof*, to mention just a few, and I wondered what, in 1958, their reaction would be to a low-budget army knock-about comedy in black and white. Little did I or any of the actors in *Carry On Sergeant*, realize that we were in at the birth of what was to become a landmark in the history of British film comedy. And now, with their continuous showing on television, they are an institution.

Reading the *Guardian*'s obituary column – I'm not morbid by nature, just curious to see if I'm in it – I read of the death of author and playwright, Bill Naughton. His passing evoked mixed feelings of sadness and very happy times. The latter came about on the one occasion we worked together, creating 'Alfie', Bill's character in the radio play of the same name. Bill had been described as an author 'with a marvellous ear for the talk of life', and the play was the mirror of a man he had worked with during the war and of whose day-to-day conversations he had taken notes. A theatre critic likened them to 'Reading your lover's diary': delightful, horrible, but always fascinating. Here are two examples of Alfie's philosophy:

> The first thing I look for on a job is the fiddle! You know what I mean? If there ain't one I ain't interested.

> It was Siddie, my regular Thursday night bint, a married woman of twenty-nine, so she said, but she could be thirty-two or three and quite a fair bit of grumble...

The play was produced by Douglas Cleverdon, a man of endless radio drama experience, including the introduction of the poet Dylan Thomas's first play, *Under Milk Wood*. So began a long haul, three weeks of rehearsal, of discovering Alfie – through his voice. Bill, ever willing to attend to try and find the answers to my endless questions, with Douglas in the shadows patiently bolstering my fluctuating enthusiasm as I sought the identity of this very particular, self-assured but pitiful human being. And so finally I created Alfie, my Alfie. And despite the novel that followed, from which came the play with John Neville and then the film with Michael Caine, Alfie was mine. I gave him birth, he belonged to me, I knew him – I was born among Alfies.

After the broadcast I received the following letter, dated 9 January 1962.

Dear Bill Owen,
I felt I really must write and congratulate you on your brilliant performance in *Alfie Elkins's Little Life*. It held me from start to finish. Your skill was such that I found it hard to believe the real Alfie was not in fact speaking. I do hope we shall be able to persuade you to do something else for us in sound broadcasting in the not so distant future.

P H Newby,

Controller, Third Programme

At the time of writing, over thirty years later, I have just received a contract informing me that *Alfie Elkins's Little Life* is to be repeated on BBC Radio 3.

8

A New Departure

Both Newhaven, Sussex and Newhaven, Connecticut have been significant for me. It was in Newhaven, Connecticut, a then small picture-postcard town typical of those I'd seen in the movies that, on 7 December 1949, at the Schubert Theater, the curtain rose on the New York Theater Guild's production of *As You Like It*. All I can say about the town's British namesake is that it somehow lacks the glamour of its American cousin, being a small commercial port with a cross-Channel ferry service. But when David King, the Leader of the Newhaven Boys' Club in Sussex asked me to open their Annual Summer Fête, I agreed to meet him and immediately felt a bond. I learned later that his marriage was falling apart. Perhaps this had been part of the mutual and instant empathy between us. But whatever the reason, our meeting began a friendship that has lasted more than thirty years. He has since retired to the country, but still comes up to London occasionally where we have lunch and talk about times past and my continuing involvement in Boys' Clubs, for which I received the MBE in 1976.

Beyond my political involvement with the Labour Party and the never-ending round of opening one function or another I had never felt the need to ally myself with a particular charity, as have many showbiz personalities. But my first visit to a boys' club changed all that. I was instantly hooked. The boys were from a similar background to mine. I could identify with and relate to them. Because this new association caused such a change in my life I think I should explain a little of my early involvement.

It all began with gentle and careful persuasion from David. First I became President of the Club, then he arranged for me to talk to the boys about the theatre and acting, which as far as they were concerned was a foreign subject and not regarded by the majority of them as an asset to their macho image. The problem was how to hold their interest and enthusiasm and at the same time rid them of any self-consciousness. Educationally they were mainly in the 'C' stream, and their individual club membership span had an average of two years, so there was no time to attempt either theory or improvisation. I had to find a play that obeyed the rules that, as I saw them, were essential: immediate identification with the characters whatever the situation, the same with the pattern of dialogue, fast action, and no longer than half an hour, and also allowing for non-speaking parts. It was the Director of the National Youth Theatre who advised me, 'You want plays like that, Bill, you will have to sit down and write them.' Which is what I did and still do.

With all my years of experience working in Boys' Clubs around the country, trying to prove the value of the performing arts, there can be no doubt that my greatest rewards and satisfaction came with the boys at Newhaven. But this is quite understandable – it was where it all began, the ideas, the experimentation, the theories and the plays. I held sessions trying to explain *how* I was trying to make them act. Yes, they got bored sometimes, but they never lost the excitement of trying to put pieces together and making them work. Behind all of this was the belief and dedication of David King, supporting me in what I was trying to achieve.

One of the highlights was reaching the finals of the Sussex British Drama League Festival held at Glyndebourne, that holy of holies of the opera buffs. We didn't win; I didn't expect us to, not against such an opposition of enthusiastic juvenile talent. The truth was my boys just couldn't behave. They had, quite early on, been ticked off by the Warden for playing football on the sacred lawns. But what angered me was the adjudication for our play. The man either failed to comprehend or purposely ignored the fact that the lads from Newhaven were not a band of keen students of drama. They were rough and tough, a reflection of their backgrounds, and had, alien as it was to their natures, performed a play that afternoon which to my mind brought the only sense of reality to the entire proceedings. They knew nothing of technique, all they needed was a word of encouragement. Seeing my annoyance, a couple of the older lads suggested they go and 'thump him'. David and I got them quickly on the bus as soon as the formalities were over!

By the time I came back to live in London in 1963 I was totally involved, having written a number of short plays and pamphlets expounding my theories and experience of drama in Boys' Clubs. I was asked to chair a panel of enthusiasts involved in this activity and toured the country giving classes whenever time permitted – as I still do. I can never fully know the results of my past, present and, hopefully, future efforts, but I can say, already, that I have been more than rewarded.

Certainly, the publication of my short plays for the National Association of Boys' Clubs proved very successful. The most successful one came about as I was browsing around for fresh ideas and came across a film script I had written years ago on the life of Dr Barnardo, to which were attached several letters of rejection from various film companies. Later I learned from a director at an end-of-film party that I was one of many who'd had the same idea, and with the same result. I heard a rumour at one time that Dickie Attenborough and Bryan Forbes were going to do a stage musical of the story, but it never happened, and the film about Barnardo's life has yet to be made. The trouble with the subject is the subject itself. It seems to be two separate stories, and the second can never match the drama of the first. We begin with Barnardo as a medical student at the London Hospital in the East End slums, where he becomes aware of the plight of hundreds of apparently parentless and homeless children who run wild, living on their wits by day and sleeping rough at night, with nothing being done for them by an uncaring government or society. This is the stuff of drama – telling of his concern, compassion, struggle and determination, including litigation, to rescue these 'street arabs', as they were called, and his fight to open his first Home. Whilst, if the latter part of the story, if memory serves me, is on the other hand concerned primarily with his acquisition of property for this purpose.

It is in the early part of the story that a young boy takes Barnardo to a warehouse in Houndsditch where he climbs a ladder to discover a number of children, aged four to fourteen, huddled together, sleeping out on the roof. Here is a quotation from one of the earlier books on his life: 'Dr Barnardo had seen enough for one night. Sick at heart he wended his way home, well nigh despairing of his kind ... but with one determination before him!' From this particular sequence came the idea that the arrival of Barnardo on the warehouse roof could be the focal point for either the beginning or the end of a play about the youngsters asleep there. Having decided that his arrival should close the action, I wrote a short play called *The Ragged School*, which was published by Macmillan Education who then took over the publication of all my short plays. I was intrigued with this idea, as simple as it may seem, of taking a single incident from a story and creating another which is entirely compatible with the original. But, on reflection, I had done it before with my first TV play, *Lysette*, a horror story about a hand puppet in the form of a beautiful doll, which had been inspired by watching *Sooty* with Tom when he was small. I realize, of course, that there is nothing startling or original about these ideas, but I had a feeling they were leading me somewhere.

Having lunch with a friend one day, my attention was held

by a large framed print of *The Laundresses* by Degas hanging over the fireplace. I wasn't familiar with the painting and no doubt my interest was partly due to the fact that laundries proliferated where I spent my childhood – indeed, the area was known as 'soapsuds island' and my mother seemed to spend half her life in such a place. The painting is of two girls, one ironing a shirt and the other yawning. It was the latter that particularly interested me. Why was she yawning? Was it the end of a hard day, or had she been out on the tiles the night before? Such questions led me to the obvious conclusion that here lay the final answer, a visual focal point where a story might either begin or end. I returned home and wrote the play, *Laundry Girls* of about thirty minutes' duration, using the yawning girl to open it. It was immediately published by Macmillan and has been reprinted several times.

This was years before Sondheim's *Sunday in the Park with George* which was never anything more than a one-act musical and should have remained so. But I was inspired by the success of *Laundry Girls* and straight away wrote two more short plays based on *On the Beach, Trouville* by Monet and *Absinthe Drinkers* by Manet, both delighting me, both not quite achieving the success of *Laundry Girls*. Then, a schoolmaster friend who had become very enthusiastic came to me with an idea for further development. He suggested that once the stress of the exams was over, he would hang a print of *The Laundresses* in each classroom which would then become the focal point for a varied curriculum: history, economics, the arts and so on. This was far beyond my wildest imaginings, particularly when he then suggested we write a textbook explaining the whole concept. But it never happened. I was too busy and he, becoming more and more frustrated with teaching finally gave up and took early retirement. But it was an exciting idea. However, all is not lost, I hope to make a film of *The Laundry Girls* in the near future.

Not long after I moved back to London, I appeared in a film

Aged six months *(above left)*, with my parents, age three *(above right)* and age five, with my father

With Brenda Bruce in *Caste* in 1947 *(above)* *(Angus McBean)* and
with Edith at the premiere of *The Mark of Cain* in 1948

With Katharine Hepburn and Cloris Leachman in *As You Like It* in 1949 *(above)* and with my friend John Metzler in Bradford, USA *(right)*

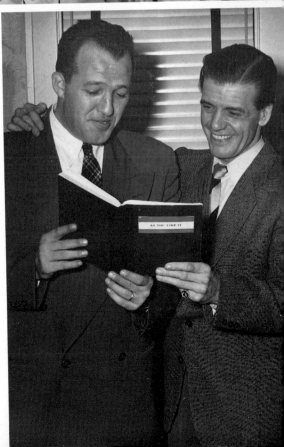

Feeding the fans

With two venerable knights on the set of *David*

The March on Russia (above) with Constance Chapman and Patsy Rowlands in 1989 *(John Haynes)*, with Brian Cox in *In Celebration* *(left)* and with T P McKenna in *The Contractor (right)*, both in 1969

With some of the lads in rehearsal
at Towcester

A proud moment – Kathie and I
outside Buckingham Palace

Nora gives a helping hand *(by courtesy of the BBC Photograph Library)*

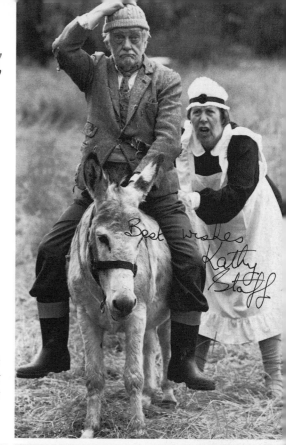

Compo, Clegg and Foggy – the original and the second trio *(left and right) (by courtesy of the BBC Photograph Library)*

Compo – surprised in a helmet *(left)* and on water skis *(right) (by courtesy of the BBC Photograph Library)*
Christmas with the cast *(by courtesy of the BBC Photograph Library)*

called *Secret of Blood Island*, a kind of mark II version of *Camp on Blood Island*, which had been a surprising box-office hit. Well, its spin-off was certainly no super-epic with a cast of thousands and a budget of millions – not with Hammer Films in the saddle!

It boasted no star names but made up for it with a bunch of reliable actors who, with good direction, were able to give some credibility to a fairly run-of-the-mill prisoner-of-war yarn. But there was some indefinable 'extra' about it that made it the flavour of the month when it was released in 1964. As with many follow-up versions to a smash hit, the plot and script are moved around but the location never changes. *Secret of Blood Island* was referred to in the pre-production blurb as a 'comparison piece' to its predecessor and it goes on to describe it as a 'full-bloodied adventure story about an Allied woman agent whose plane crashes in a steaming jungle hell'. She is found by a British prisoner-of-war working party who smuggle her into their camp, but tension and excitement mounts as the Japanese Commandant's suspicions grow – no fool, he! The notice concludes with 'This is a tough, hard-hitting, blood-and-guts subject', so we at least had an inkling of what the 'indefinable quality' might be before we started.

What I best remember about making this movie are the difficulties caused by a developing difference between the leading players, who included Jack Hedley, Lee Montague, Charles Tingwell, Michael Ripper, yours truly and the many non-speaking actors playing similar prisoner-of-war roles. When I say difference, I don't mean of status or personality, but one of appearance. Obviously the casting director had taken a great deal of trouble in choosing his non-speaking actors, selecting them for their lean and hungry look – not too difficult to come by when the phone rings but rarely! However, putting modesty to one side for a moment, I have to say that talent is taken into consideration when casting the leading players who are *ipso facto* usually in work, in funds and – dare I say it? – fatter. Not that I would use that description

when referring to Lee Montague, well, not to his face. Then
there was my old buddy, Michael Ripper who, like me,
does give the impression of not being tall; consequently any
additional poundage tends to show like a barrel of bitter where
one's stomach should be.

In other words, there was an obvious difference in the
camp – that of physique. Of course Michael will vehemently
deny he had a 'pot', whilst I readily admit to the presence of
mine. I did try dieting but its effect only began to show
towards the end of filming. Hiding mine became something of
a director's nightmare, that's probably why I had so many
close-ups! But it wasn't so obvious when I wore a shirt. I also
tried acting without breathing and I've known some actors
who have achieved this throughout their careers, but in a
colour film one's face tends to take on the complexion of a
strawberry. But this wasn't the kind of film one had time to
prepare for, shot in six weeks at Walton-on-Thames, jungle
and all.

Edith and I had been living in Brighton for about five years,
successfully acting out a reputation in that incestuous little
social whirl as the hosts with the most on the ball. But with
the departure of the last guest we took off our masks, the
farce was over and in silence I would empty the ashtrays and
Edith would go to her room.

Edith suddenly suggested we move house and I have never
been sure why. Was it a last desperate attempt to save our
marriage which had been faltering for longer than I now care
to remember? But whatever the reason, I refused to entertain
the idea. Nevertheless, she simply went out one morning and
bought a large Regency house in nearby Lewes Crescent. It
was an awe-inspiring residence with the ground floor and
basement converted into separate apartments. Eventually, of
course, I moved, despite my unheeded protestations. By now
I was accustomed to going with the flow and any so-called
resolution on my part soon crumbled. With the exception of

a small flat on the top floor which had been reserved for the housekeeper, the rest was 'home'. So a kind of peace settled between us for a while. Edith was to find great contentment in slowly returning her new home to its former glory. She indulged herself to the full – furnishings, fabrics and antiques – each room taking on its own particular Regency grandeur. The result was magnificent and she was deservedly proud of her accomplishment. Every acquisition became the topic for much speculation and admiration, each a conversation piece in our little social whirl. For example, the hanging of a Dresden chandelier in the sitting room brought about what can only be described as an upper-class tupperware party, the sound of popping champagne corks replacing the bubbling noise of percolating coffee. In the meantime I had found refuge in a little room I'd discovered. This I used as an office and study where I settled to outdo Chekhov, Ibsen or even Philip King, the most modest playwright I ever met.

News of the house got to the glossy magazines. I have before me a photograph of myself standing in front of a huge marble fireplace; Edith sits dutifully by my side, working her petit point, a crystal candelabrum stands on a nineteenth-century hand-painted grand piano. The reason why I remember this photograph is because the photographer was interrupted by a phone call for me from my accountant telling me the bank had refused a loan that would have enabled me to pay the surtax on Edith's income. As for me, I hadn't sufficient funds to renew the insurance on my car.

It was at one of the obligatory Brighton social gatherings that I was introduced to Charles Rogers, a BBC Opera producer who asked if I would be interested in playing Ko-Ko in a Sadlers Wells Opera production of *The Mikado*. Without disclosing the fact that I had never seen or heard a Gilbert and Sullivan operetta, I immediately expressed an interest. An appointment was made at Sadlers Wells to meet the director, who began the conversation by informing me that this 1963 production was a revival of one performed a year or so before.

My cautious reaction was that I hoped this would not restrict any ideas I might have of playing the character. He hastened to assure me that within the framework of the present production, he would welcome any ideas I might have. He then went on to give details of the 'impressive performance' of the previous actor who had played Ko-Ko, whose name escapes me, and who had evidently rendered one song whilst swinging back and forth on a rope. I informed him that my Ko-Ko would have very little to do with gymnastics. I had already acquainted myself fully with the score and libretto and had an instinctive reaction that I was going to make my Ko-Ko 'an original'. I gave my audition and sang 'Tit Willow' which seemed to go down quite well. The 'Big Boss' laughed – it was supposed to be a sad little song!

Once again I was tackling a heavy musical score, but this time in the company of opera singers, including Marion Studholme, Patricia Kern, Gwynne Howell and David Hellman. When we all gathered for the first morning's rehearsal, I may have had my inferiority complex showing. But they were a great crowd and went out of their way to put me at my ease.

Some of them had been in the original production and their confidence seemed to rub off on me. We shared a two- or three-week tour with a new production of *Carmen*, which included Leeds and Cardiff, and there was no doubt my Ko-Ko was very popular, particularly with Earnest Bradbury, the music and opera critic of the *Yorkshire Post* who also happened to be an ardent Savoyard and knew his Gilbert and Sullivan to the placing of a final comma.

... Bill Owen's Ko-Ko [is] quite literally an upstart tailor straight from the East End. This is the jewel of the production. He comes on after a most dramatic build-up, shyly, nervously putting one twisted leg before the other in a tremendous effort to accustom himself to his new and lordly position, not strong enough to lift the executioner's axe. At one point in his soliloquy, he jumps quickly back to his natural element, cross-legged, threading an invisible needle with the professional dexterity of a lifetime...

Bill Owen's entry as Ko-Ko was the most glorious single moment I have experienced in the theatre for many years. I don't think I shall ever forget it!

In the early hours of the day of the London opening I was informed by telephone of my mother's death. I went to her as quickly as I could and, with the help of a neighbour and the doctor, managed to attend to all those sad but necessary details that we all have to face at some time or other in our lives. I hadn't seen my father when he was dead and the doctor was somewhat bewildered when I refused his invitation to disturb the peace of that darkened front room where my mother lay at rest. Are there two more important people in one's life? I don't think so, not when they gave you the love and understanding that I'd had.

I rang Sadlers Wells and explained that under the circumstances I would be unable to make the dress rehearsal. They were kind, suggesting that the understudy was quite adequate if I preferred not to play the opening. After all, was it right that a loving son should be clowning on stage trying to make people laugh at such a time? But what else could I do? I had nowhere else to go.

Following an otherwise happy time with Sadlers Wells, I was asked to partner Sid James in a new BBC TV series, *Taxi*, by Ted Willis, which concerned the adventures of a London cab and its joint owners. It also included an up-and-coming young actor by the name of Ray Brookes. It was a thirteen-part series which necessitated my staying in London – well that was my excuse. I would stay in town Monday to Friday and go back to Brighton at weekends. One Monday morning at Brighton station I met Nina, a company secretary, also going to work in London. We spoke as we waited for the train and so our relationship began.

I was divorced by Edith after eighteen years of marriage; our
parting was inevitable, we had become almost like strangers. I
remember on our way to some social occasion she broke our
usual silence saying, 'Say something to me, Bill.' It was almost
as if she were pleading with me, and all I could reply was, 'I
can't think of anything to say.' And I meant it. I duly removed
myself and my few belongings from our museum of a house.
And I recall being back in London, looking at the small pile
of personal belongings in my room – books, records, clothes,
typewriter etc. – and reflecting that this was the sum total of
my effects when I got married! What had happened in between?
The only stake I could claim was that of father to our son,
and I would probably lose him with the divorce. Where *does*
all the love go?

So there I was, a divorce on my hands and nowhere to live;
I've had better scenarios! And Nina accepted it all with her
quiet enthusiasm, something I have to admit I didn't share at
the time. But that was the great thing about her, she had this
almost chameleon-like quality of being able to adapt to any
circumstance. For example, for one who was not involved
with the theatre until she met me, she became not only an
enthusiastic playgoer but was immediately at ease in the
company of actors and a perfect audience for all our off-stage
performances!

One day Jack Grossman – a film maker and writer whom I
had met when we worked together on a fringe production of
Whiten Your Fanlight (a quote from a government pamphlet
on protection against the atomic bomb!) – phoned offering me
a couple of days' work on a documentary he was making.
There was something else: he'd heard that Nina and I had to
get out of the room in Upper Wimpole Street where we'd been
lodging, and he offered us the temporary use of a put-u-up
settee in his Kilburn flat. A friend in need is a friend under
any circumstances! It was a large flat – it needed to be, Jack's
wife, Vera, was enormous with child, besides which they were
also sheltering Kathie, another orphan from another collapsed

marriage. If you wanted privacy you went to bed, but even Nina and I were able to postpone that temptation in order to enjoy the ritual of the evening meal, when we all gathered around the kitchen table and exchanged the day's happenings over fish and chips or a Chinese take-away, washed down with cheap plonk. Five people living on top of one another, in harmony and sharing so much laughter.

Hilarious is a good one-word description of that time, particularly the weekday ablutions when, with the exception of Vera, we all had to get to work. Come Sundays, however, things were different. Jack and I took our time, allowing the four ladies to attend to their toilette. Yes, four. We had acquired a friend of Vera's who'd had a fight with her husband – and lost. But from this ménage came an experience for Jack, which I have persuaded him to relate...

'It was 9.00 a.m. on a dull Sunday morning when the doorbell rang and I crept to the front door, bleary-eyed, and concerned to make sure the rest of the 'guests' weren't disturbed, as we'd all been up late the night before putting the world to rights. I inched the door open, to be greeted by a smiling black gentleman, accompanied by an earnest-looking young white lady, who clutched a swatch of the latest edition of News from the Other World. I was about to say "I'm sorry, but we already have one of those" when a foot – or was it a Bible? – was thrust purposefully into the gap I'd left while answering the door.

' "Good Sabbath, will you spare a few moments of your time for the Lord, sir?" the smiling face said. "We are here to spread the good news about Jesus Christ," he went on, applying pressure to widen the gap in the door.

'Not wishing to offend, I said quickly, "I'm Jewish." Expecting at the very least a subtle allusion to my personal responsibility for the crucifixion, the information acted, not as a deterrent, but as a challenge for my conversion which would win extra brownie points back at HQ. Deftly flicking to a bookmarked section of the Old Testament in his all-purpose

Bible, he began to quote at length from Samuel, Chapter 7, Verse 8, or the like. My knowledge of the Bible is sketchy. I can just about recall a section or two, learned parrot-fashion for my barmitzvah, but something about the evangelist's persistence struck an obstinate chord in me. I'm known as a competent improviser, so I responded with confident counter-quotations from Ecclesiastes which I made up as I went along.

'The evangelist began searching frantically for the quotation, while the lady helper seemed to be saying a silent prayer for her colleague to respond quickly, to regain the initiative. He swiftly found another bookmarked quotation of his own, but as he read it, his attention began to waver as he became aware of the activity going on behind me. The first of the female entourage was making her way slowly to the bathroom. His eyes widened and his concentration faltered as the seemingly endless procession to and from the toilet of a variety of nightdress-clad ladies passed his field of vision. His companion's eyes narrowed and they exchanged glances. At first puzzled, but quickly realizing the implications, I tried to keep the conversation going with more plausible-sounding biblical quotes. Finally, the appearance of Vera, now several months' pregnant, paddling across the hall was too much for the evangelists. Concluding that I was running a harem in North West London, the Bible was snapped shut and the pair beat a hasty retreat. As I later told Bill, I was quite disappointed and was just beginning to enjoy the cut and thrust of biblical discourse!'

We actors are really very sensitive creatures, I might almost say fragile. A telephone that remains silent too long can bring on the deepest depression. Then, it's: 'I'm finished, they've forgotten my name,' followed by the usual accusation: 'Useless bloody agent, I'll get a new one,' and so on. Then, just as one starts making enquiries about driving a mini-cab or stacking shelves at Tesco's, the phone rings – maybe.

It wasn't the telephone for me, but a thick, large envelope

dropping through the letter box. I could tell with that extra-
sensory perception actors develop over the years that it contained a script. Enclosed was a letter from a management
whose name I can't remember, asking if I would care to act
in it with a short tour prior to its opening in a West End
theatre. As always, that old feeling of self-confidence returned.
Would I care to do it? There was still someone out there who
assumed I was overwhelmed with offers. What the hell was I
worrying about the bank manager for? I read the play and
resumed worrying about the bank manager.

Described by its author, a Hungarian like the author of *The
Trap* (of blessed memory), as a comedy, the play was called
The Importance of Being Dressed. I re-read it and for some
unknown reason I kept being reminded of Sunderland and an
almost empty theatre with a strange youth reading a comic in
the front row. My only recollection of the play was the high
spot when my trousers fell down! Or were they Ian Shand's?
Ian got into the play by mistake when he'd accompanied his
girlfriend, Freda Knor, who was auditioning for the part of
my wife, and she had rehearsed the scene with him. She was
excellent but far too young and attractive. Ian was also very
good, so he was given the other leading role! There was a
rumour that Freda thumped him when they got outside, but
I'm glad they both came along because with Jack Grossman they
are to be counted amongst my nearest and dearest friends. The
play? A disaster. It should have stayed in Hungary. Losing your
trousers is good for a laugh – I speak from experience of *Last
of the Summer Wine* – but never as a denouement!

In 1859 a new play by Ivan Aleksandrovich Goncharov entitled
Oblomov was given its Moscow première and the critics
described it as a classic, finding in it 'many symbols of the
Russian gentry', or 'an illness fostered by the nature of the
Slavonic character and the life of Russian society'. The story
concerns an indolent young man who feels that a life of lying
in bed and doing nothing is a more meaningful way of spending

time than rushing about in pursuit of wealth, position or power. But when faced with love, in the shape of Olga Ilyinska Sergeyevna, he finds he is incapable of returning it and goes back to his negative existence.

It was on this classic story of Goncharov's that Riccardo Aragno based his play, also with the title *Oblomov*, and Michael White acquired the production rights with Frank Dunlop to direct as a vehicle for Spike Milligan. It turned out to be the most bizarre theatrical experience of my long and varied career. I played Zakhar, manservant to Oblomov, an aged peasant of few manners and many nasty habits, including total disdain for his master, whilst Madame Olga Sergeyevna, the lady who confronts Oblomov with love, was played by Joan Greenwood. These were the three main characters around whom the story revolved. There were several minor roles played by good actors, including Marjie Lawrence, Ian Flintoff and Valentine Dyall.

Spike's theatrical experience was limited. It was *The Goon Show* that had made him such a popular comedian, along with Peter Sellers and Harry Secombe. Their maniacal brilliance had made them unique. I remember starring in *Happy Holiday* a radio show with Dennis Price, neither of us very experienced in radio comedy, which became very apparent when Peter made his only appearance in the show with a regular five-minute spot, and in that short time turned our rather timid little entertainment into a riot. Anything following became an anti-climax!

Rehearsals began and it soon became clear they might become a little tedious because Spike, quite understandably, found difficulty in learning such a script. But patience was shown by all, particularly by the director, and I had plenty of time to think about Zakhar. I began to know him down to the last button on his shirt; playing him was going to be a doddle – or so I thought. On 7 October 1964, at the Lyric Theatre, Hammersmith, before an expectant audience, Spike made his début in a classical role and within a half-hour of the curtain going up I knew the play was sinking fast. He was way out of his depth and when he called to me as I was about to exit: 'I hope Milton Shulman's not in tonight,' I knew panic had set in.

The press was not, how shall I put it, impressed. Here are a few headlines: 'A bizarre dialogue in monotone' (*Daily Mail*); 'Spike Milligan in a strait-jacket' (*The Scotsman*); 'A treat for connoisseurs of Milligan' (*Evening Standard*); 'Goonery can't save this' (*Daily Worker*). And, somewhat patronizingly, I thought, the *New Daily* commented, 'A play bound to improve'.

I think Max Madden in *Tribune* put it succinctly when he wrote: 'One could almost hear Spike reminding himself to be serious throughout this adaptation of the famous Russian novel.'

But all of this made very little difference to the box office which had within a few days sold every seat for the entire six-week run. Oblomov, Schmoblomov! These were Milligan fans and there were a lot of them – he could have packed the Palladium playing the Yellow Pages! However, it was obvious that he couldn't carry the responsibility of this classic role and immediately began to shed himself of it, so by the end of the first week it was beginning to look like Oblomov playing Milligan. Michael White asked if Joan and I would go along with this, and we both agreed to. But I had already come to the conclusion that if I was to survive amid the anarchy of this Milliganese, then I had to establish very firmly and fast that I had not joined this play to be a stooge. If it was comedy we were after, I too had had plenty of practice and, to quote Ernie Wise, 'When your turn comes ...' and I expected Spike to respect that. It took time and patience but we made it work and those weeks at the Lyric were quite the most hilarious I've ever experienced.

Having rid himself of any pretence at serious acting – every night the play would change – Spike took every serious situation and turned it on its head.

An example or two...

TARENTYEV (*played by Valentine Dyall referring to Oblomov's lawyer*) Why do you waste your time with that financial leech?

SPIKE   Well, he's in the play and he's cheap!

(OLGA *played by Joan Greenwood mimes playing the harpsichord to a recording.*)

GUEST I don't know, Olga, but you played that tonight as you've never played before.

SPIKE   With the lid up!

DOCTOR (*Ian Flintoff*) Whatever you do, you must avoid passion.

SPIKE   I do, I always travel by bus!

SPIKE   (*referring to Zakhar*) He's getting old, his legs fell off yesterday!

One night, Spike made a great performance of crossing his legs, during which one of his slippers flew into the audience. He rose slowly, walked down to the front of the stage and said to a very large lady in the front row: 'Madam, unless you have three legs, can I have my slipper back?'

We transferred to the Comedy Theatre with a new title, *Son of Oblomov*. Well, why not, we had a new play! Riccardo Aragno threatened to sue Michael White, not as you might imagine on artistic grounds because of the mutilation of his play, but for the sordid reason of money! It was a riotous opening night and the critics certainly played a different tune: 'Inspired lunacy' (*Daily Mirror*); 'A superb clown at work' (*The Sun*); 'In praise of Milligan' (*Observer*); 'Milligan, maniac and marvel' (*Daily Mail*).

The word 'genius' was in the air, and when the Queen, on her thirty-ninth birthday, was invited by Princess Anne, along with other members of the Royal Family to see the show, the seal of success was upon us and we were set for a long run. However, we now had a situation where the 'play' more or less relied on the improvisation, spontaneous wit or whatever you cared to call it of one person – Spike. This sometimes made it difficult, to say the least, for the other actors. For instance, the sentimental scenes between Joan and Spike became almost farcical and I remember well the night she and I waited to take our curtain call when she rested her head on my shoulder and whispered, 'I'm sorry, Bill, I can't take it any more.' She left the play and was replaced by her understudy who played for the rest of the run. Nevertheless, certain extremely funny situations did develop between Spike and me, which, through my persistence, became a continuous part of the play.

Having had little or no theatrical experience, and of the discipline required for the sustaining of a character over a long period, it was inevitable, certainly in these circumstances, that his efforts to raise a laugh would become increasingly frantic. He would make remarks regarding a fellow actor's performance during a scene, he'd invite members of the audience on to the stage where they would be left to become an embarrassment. As brilliant as his repartee with the audience could be, there were times when, as on a Friday or Saturday, when some of his more exuberant fans had a bellyful of beer, it could develop into a heated argument and Spike would have to leave the stage in order to allow things to cool down and let the play continue. I was told of an incident after I had left the show, when he not only left the stage, but also the theatre and went home! I understand it was a war wound which left him with recurring chronic black depressions when he was unable to perform. During such times Valentine Dyall took over the role of Oblomov. Valentine was a well-known and respected actor, but it was a disaster simply because we didn't have a play any more. It was a weird, sometimes enjoyable, but often exceedingly frustrating experience.

There was more clutter around about this time when I appeared as a guest panellist on the TV quiz show, *Tell the Truth*, a sort of poor man's *What's My Line?*, and as a consequence was offered a regular seat on the panel, which included Frances Day with David Jacobs as chairman. Suddenly I had the taste for telly, money for old rope. Then John Irwin, 'king' of the quiz presenters, offered me my own show, *Keep It in the Family*. I can't remember much about it, which, let me add, was also the case on its first showing when I forgot the rules! In fact the calamities of live TV became a favourite topic of conversation among actors at that time – Robert Adams, as Othello, collapsed during a soliloquy and another actor clammed up with nerves and had to be prompted throughout the entire play. Then cameras became mobile by placing them on manoeuvrable trolleys with bicycle wheels. There was one occasion when I was appearing in *Saloon Bar*, when two such cameras became locked together. It was during the final scene when all was about to be revealed and I can see that poor actor's face to this day. The terror of performing on TV in those days was very real, with everything going out live. The nerves, the panic! How did we ever manage to give a performance?

John Irwin gave me a second chance and I got it right that time. Very soon the show was in the charts. Coincidentally, it was then that Gilbert Harding, a man who had made his reputation simply by being bloody-minded and rude on *What's My Line?* became, as a consequence, TV critic for the *People* and decided to pile insult and vilification upon us like some old maid:

> Just as a rabbit cannot tear its horrified eyes from the fearful fascination of the weasel, time after time I have found myself compelled to go on looking at the most degrading programme that television has yet contrived!

Then he had a go at the competitors:

> Shame and embarrassment relieved by explosive giggles seem to have wiped out the last trace of intelligence. It can't

surely be true that people enjoy making such a spectacle of themselves for the entertainment of others.

But wait! There are two more panel games in which I was involved, *Laugh Line* and *Dad You're a Square*. I plead guilty, m'lud and promise never to do it again. I didn't!

9

Love, Lyrics and Lindsay Anderson

The relationship between actor and agent depends on just how much work the agent can get for his client. I have never liked changing agents, I find it embarrassing and with no guarantees as to its effectiveness. Such changes have been rare in my life, but I have to admit that around the early sixties I found myself blessed with one who was seldom available after lunch since he was thereafter closeted at his club or in consultation with his bookmaker. Thus I felt the time had come for a change and rang Michael Sullivan.

Michael was a variety agent with aspirations to having 'legitimate' clients. I became his first and to my knowledge only actor on his books. We had met socially, he was quite a fan and had already broached the subject of representing me. When I say he was a fan I'm not kidding. At social gatherings, interviews with impresarios, wherever and to whomsoever, he would announce, 'Don't worry about Bill, he can act anything!' He was a good friend and a hustler; I have never met anyone in my life who had as much faith in me, and by the heck didn't he make me live up to it! For example, I saw both the play and film of *Who's Afraid of Virginia Woolf?* and not for one second did I relate myself to the character of George, played in the movie by Richard Burton, opposite his then wife Elizabeth Taylor as Martha. Written by Edward Albee, it's a difficult play, and

128

one I can best describe as a horror movie about a marital relationship.

The offer to play George came at very short notice and, having read the play, my suspicions were aroused that perhaps a previous actor had also come to my conclusion as to the impossibility of the task and backed off. This was not a West End production, let me add, but part of the repertory season at the Wimbledon Theatre, an Edwardian edifice in South London.

It was rather 'heavy' for their usual season of popular plays, but the terms were the same, two weeks' rehearsal and two weeks' playing. I sat opposite the company manager as he laid down the terms. I asked myself how anyone was going to be able to put the play on in two weeks? But my thoughts were interrupted by the indefatigable Michael – you've guessed – 'Don't worry, Arthur, Bill can act anything!'

I had a week in which to try to discover both the heart of the play and the soul of George and Martha's relationship before rehearsals began. Martha was to be played by Jessica Dunning, a dear sweet woman, who proved to have the patience of Job during the first week's rehearsal, as did the director, John Gordon Ash. But it wasn't a happy week for me, I couldn't even get George into first gear and come Friday evening John suggested that we work together over the weekend. This I had to decline as it was Tommy's 'visiting' Sunday.

The sixties saw in the Beatles, Flower Power, Sexual Equality and my divorce. Quite rightly, Edith had been given custody of Tom who was by now a young teenager at Lancing College and, sensitive to the closeness of my relationship with him, she readily agreed to any reasonable arrangements for access that I cared to make.

Nina and I were now living in a flat in Marylebone High Street where, for propriety's sake, we had all agreed Tom could visit but not stay overnight. Inevitably that rule went the way of so many in life, and along with that came my son's declaration that he no longer wanted to live with Edith, he wanted to stay with us. And what's more, as if the cat wasn't already among the pigeons, he stated that he didn't want to stay on at Lancing. To put it mildly, these were added problems I could have well done without. Wounds that had hardly had time to heal were sure to be opened again. And they were. I eventually had to phone Edith, and to say she was shocked would be an understatement. She'd had no intimation whatsoever of Tom's feelings or intentions. When she asked to speak to him, he refused. So I became the culprit and curses and accusations were rained upon my head – for the second time! A very chastened offspring was sent to bed with the order 'Get your arse back to Lancing tomorrow morning smartish! Tell your headmaster I'll be phoning. Goodnight!' This havoc had begun almost with his arrival, it was now nine o'clock at night and I hadn't even thought of George or Martha or bloody Virginia Woolf. Nina began to weep; I opened a bottle.

It was at rehearsal the following day, while I was still suffering the effects of 'Bloody Sunday', when John Gordon Ash rushed up to me from the stalls shouting, 'Bill, Bill, you've found him, you must have worked like hell over the weekend, it's great!' Then, over a quiet drink at lunchtime, Jessica enquired, 'Something happened over the weekend?'

'It most certainly did,' I replied.

'I won't pry,' she said. 'But I think you should know, you frightened the life out of me this morning.'

So it seemed I had found George, or George had found me, but there had to be an easier way.

If I learned anything from Tom, it was surely this: never underestimate the resilience of your children. Mind you, I might have known, having already experienced this 'innocence' once before, shortly after his mother and I had parted. I had visited the college and then taken Tom to lunch at a Worthing hotel. We were having coffee in the lounge when he suddenly burst into tears, something I hadn't expected and, riddled with

guilt, I could almost feel the accusing eyes of the other guests –
'What *has* that man done to make that dear boy sob his heart
out?' In an effort to relieve the situation, I went for the
obvious. 'Is there anything you want?' I whispered. He stopped
crying and replied, 'Yes I have to get some sugar for the
dorm's late-night cocoa.'

One morning my agent Michael phoned – it was before nine
o'clock, a sure sign that there had been an emergency which
he had resolved with his 'Bill can act anything' routine! It
seemed that ill health had forced Sydney Tafler, playing
Captain de Treville in *The Four Musketeers*, to leave the
show suddenly, and I was to 'get down to the Theatre Royal'
as soon as I could. I was welcomed by the company manager
who explained the situation again. He then gave me a script
to read, which I didn't, having managed to discover the part
of Captain de Treville and not being very impressed. I was
then introduced to Peter Coe, the director, who in turn
introduced me to the company – who applauded! Then Peter
informed me that Joyce Blackham had left the show due to
the fact that her big song had been cut. I had a sense of
foreboding.

I have little or no recollection of Captain de Treville as a
character, but rather as a vehicle which, with the full co-
operation of my dear friend Harry Secombe, I could at least
make an impression. This I obviously did, because after the
first dress rehearsal, which ran over four hours, the first
observation was from Bernard (later Lord) Delfont, the impresario, remarking with an air of panic, 'You're not going to
play him like that, Bill, are you?' But before I could offer a
reason, excuse or drop to my knees for absolution, Peter called
a company meeting because he had to cut more than an hour
from the show.

As we settled in our seats I looked about me and got the
distinct impression that this was not the first of such meetings
that had taken place during rehearsals, and I shall never forget

the look of total resignation on the face of bold Aramio, played by John Junkin! As you can imagine, slicing an hour from a show is not so much cutting as performing an amputation. My sense of foreboding deepened and was finally proved justified. Slowly but surely the role of Captain de Treville was reduced to the equivalent of a foot soldier in *War and Peace*. Then, to my amazement, and to the amazement of the rest of the cast, I sprang to my feet and told them so, adding that this was not the role that I had accepted and my contract was no longer valid. Peter Coe agreed, perhaps a little too enthusiastically, I thought, and I was on my way to the stage door when Bernard Delfont hurried after me. Please note that, *hurried* after me! He then politely offered me a generous financial reparation. To this day I've never been able to figure out whether it was generosity or relief! Michael left the country soon after, without explanation...

Now, if you are beginning to think matters had reached a low ebb, I can tell you they came to an even sorrier pass! Nothing at that time seemed to be going right. The musical *Queenie* by Lord Willis, with Paul Eddington, Vivien Martin and yours truly had folded within a few weeks.

In the meantime there came the advent of commercial television, and countless small companies were springing up, all trying to edge their way into television advertising. Whatever their professed expertise, very few knew anything about acting or actors or, in some instances, good manners. There's a story about Fay Compton, a huge star in her day, being interviewed for a commercial by some young upstart whose opening gambit was, 'OK, Miss Compton, tell me what you've done.' Fay leant across his desk and said 'No, you tell me what you've done!'

I had two such interviews, one began with an ignorant little twit throwing a pencil in my lap, saying, 'Go on then, g'is a laugh outa dat!' Then Anthony Newley stood me up for over an hour regarding a new show he was putting on at the Prince of Wales Theatre and when he did finally arrive, he hadn't a clue what the appointment was for! By the second post I received a tax demand, and the final curtain fell when I had another interview for a commercial where the 'director' introduced himself with, ' 'Ere, 'old 'ard, you don't look a bit like your photo in *Spotlight*!' I'd had enough, I blew it: 'That's because I have to meet little amateur shits like you every day!' Exit lines like that are very few and far between.

When I got back to my flat I reached for the bottle and it wasn't long before I was well on the way to slipping off the couch. Then, out of my alcoholic haze, came a decision. 'Give it up, you don't have to suffer these indignities' and I began to cry! But let me add in my defence that this was not some wild, drunken impulse. I have always vowed that this profession would never give me up – leaving it would always be my choice. I put the bottle away, cooked some supper and went to bed.

The next morning I wrote a letter to the Principal of the North-Western College of Speech and Drama where, because of my experience with boys' clubs, I had given several lectures to student teachers, and I asked if there was a possibility of such lectures becoming a regular part of the curriculum.

That same morning I received a phone call on behalf of Hazel Vincent Wallace, an ex-Unity Theatre actress who was then running the Leatherhead Theatre. She wanted to hear the Tony Russell score to my new musical version of *Matchgirls*.

'What does it feel like, Bill, to know that you're going to make a hundred grand?' That was the question put to me by John Franz, a top record producer at Phillips during a session with Harry Secombe recording 'I Long to See the Day', a song from the musical *Matchgirls*. It certainly looked as though Tony and I were going to hit the jackpot with this show, and it hadn't even opened in London yet! A fairy story that very nearly came true.

This is probably the right time to put the fairy story on 'hold' and deal with the grim realities of the subject – this brief, but important moment of industrial history. The first recorded women's industrial dispute, which took place in 1888. The original play by Robert Mitchell had dealt mainly with the social and industrial issues, which included what would be politely termed as 'health hazards'. In those days they went with the job! For instance, phosphorus, a toxic ingredient, is essential in the making of matches, but when the 'dinner break' came round there were no facilities for the girls to wash their hands before eating. So they ate as they were, and where they worked. In doing so they exposed themselves to the very real possibility of eating contaminated food, setting up an infection known as 'phossy jaw' – actually gangrene of the jawbone resulting in terrible facial disfigurement and, sometimes, death. There was also a system of petty fines for, say, having dirty feet or talking at work, but the main complaint was the wages which Bryant and May first gave as sixteen to seventeen shillings per week, later admitting to a figure nearer eleven shillings, which, however, after further investigation was found in some cases to be as low as six shillings. So the girls went on strike under the guidance of Annie Besant, a Fabian and champion of many causes, resulting in victory for them with the directors acceding to all their demands.

I first met Tony during the fringe revue *Whiten Your Fanlight*, for which he wrote the music. He played trombone in the John Dankworth band and had written several pieces for John. But it was in the musical story form where he was to discover and extend his creative ability. The partnership between composer and writer is always a gamble, but as long as good songs are being created, who cares if they hate the sight of each other? Of course there have been great partnerships that just happened, who could have thought that Richard Rodgers would find another partner after Lorenz Hart! Yet when Oscar Hammerstein II died, Rodgers is quoted as saying 'It's like losing your right arm.' But Jay Lerner could never repeat the success he'd had with Fritz Loewe. Cole Porter never needed a partner! Then there were those great writers and composers who could work with anyone of stature, Johnny Mercer,

Burton Lane, André Previn or Stephen Sondheim. They all shared what I believe to be basic in collaboration – the grace to know when it's time to bend a little.

As far as I can remember Tony and I had no system for working together. The subject of the Matchgirls' strike had been with me since that Sunday afternoon at Unity Theatre during the blitz when I saw that heroic performance. I had rewritten and produced it again in 1948 and since then I had resisted any persuasion to adapt it to musical form, until I met Tony. Even then one could hardly describe our partnership as producing a great flood of inspiration. I think we worked together, off and on, for about four years before we were satisfied.

In order to accommodate music and songs, the libretto had to be rewritten. I introduced Bernard Shaw who was vaguely involved, mainly through Annie Besant with whom it was rumoured he had a romance. However, nowhere in his writings or correspondence is her name even mentioned. But during my earlier research I read of some scandal where she is said to have stood outside his house screaming for the return of her letters. He was also to refer to her as 'someone who wishes to act out a succession of dramatic roles'. Someone else involved in this 'fairy story' was Gillian Lynne, who directed and choreographed the show, and for whom it did come true, providing her with the turning point in her career which has made her today arguably the most popular modern cho-reographer in the world. To date she has ten productions of both *Cats* and *Phantom of the Opera* to her credit – making her probably the richest, too! It was premièred at the Leatherhead Theatre, a small converted cinema, cosseted and cared for by Hazel, who remembered the original play and was very excited at the prospect of presenting the show. A nostalgic trip for us both.

It was a trifle cramped for both audience and actors. How Gillian ever got it on that stage I'll never know – part of the band was out in the corridor. But what a first night! What a reception! Nina got a little tipsy and cried, she was so overcome and happy. I got drunk after I'd had three firm offers to take it into town. The fairy story had begun. Within forty-eight hours the word was 'around the town'. What was happening down at Leatherhead? Some London dailies were running features. I was offered £20,000 for the music rights by an American who seemed very frustrated because he couldn't 'buy a piece of the action'. Every seat in the house was sold for the entire three-week run. By the time the final curtain had fallen there had been fourteen offers to open the show in town and one for a New York première prior to London! We had to have a meeting to decide who was going to be the lucky one.

Matchgirls opened at the Globe Theatre, Shaftesbury Avenue on 1 March 1966. So the story that began for me on a cold winter afternoon during the blitz, with a heroic performance in an almost roofless theatre in the darkened backstreets behind King's Cross Station, had, twenty-five years later, been fêted into the West End. The pre-publicity had been enormous, the LP of the show had been recorded and already the radio was busy with the songs. I was making guest appearances on everybody's show, as were Gillian and Tony. A Bond Street hairdresser invented the 'Matchgirl look' for his lady clients – and the press just lapped it up. On the first night everyone who was anyone was there, including, unusually, several leading politicians, both left and right. Yet it could hardly be described as a theatre establishment opening – a story about a women's strike? And, as Herbert Kretzmer dubbed it, 'an angry musical'. What's more it had a comparatively unknown cast, a description fitting the professional track record of both author and composer! At Leatherhead there had been an intimacy between the performers and the audience, a magical excitement created by Gillian's choreography and production, the very atmosphere was charged.

The auditorium of the Globe Theatre, however, seemed vast by comparison, the magic appeared to have evaporated. The anger was still there, no compromises were made, but it told

of an age that was light years away from *The Pyjama Game*,
for example, which also tells of a strike, but had all the
standard ingredients required for a commercial success – fun
songs, love songs, hit songs. Damn it, the curtain had only
been up fifteen minutes and the Matchgirls were already telling
Annie Besant, the great social worker:

> Have you ever seen a girl
> What's old before she's young?
> 'Ave you ever seen two eyes so tired
> They couldn't cry a tear?
> 'Ave you ever seen a head so bowed
> It never sees the sky?
> Look around, dear lady, look around!

But as Milton Shulman felt it necessary to point out:

> What's the point of lyrics drawing attention to their haggard
> and pitiful state when they are prancing about as if they
> had been reared on a diet of miracle vitamins and potent
> Mexican jumping beans.

The left-wing press loved it, of course, but the establishment
on the whole were not happy, even a little patronizing perhaps,
with the exception of Kretzmer who seemed deeply offended
by my 'false rhymes'. But enough is enough, it was past
midnight and the golden coach had turned back into a
pumpkin. I didn't make a hundred grand, *Matchgirls* was off
within three months and I had come to the conclusion that if
I ever had anything to do with that story again it would have
to be for the new Unity Theatre. That's where it belonged, it
is part of its history as well as the history of those brave
women who knew when it was their turn to stand and
fight. But now, almost thirty years after that disappointment,
Matchgirls remains one of the most popular musicals in play
publisher Samuel French's catalogue, with amateur performances played from Land's End to John o'Groats via Berlin
and Singapore!

While on the subject of *Matchgirls*, I am reminded of the incident when we lost Lord Gladstone's statue. It was accepted with all the publicity surrounding the show, from its opening to its last night, that relations between ourselves and the directors of the Bryant and May Match Co., now regarded as model employers, could hardly be described as cordial. But after the show's closure while there was talk of making it into a film, there was, perhaps because of a change in their public relations department, a change in Bryant and May's attitude towards myself as the author. So it was whilst down at the factory in Bow, researching through their ancient archives, engravings, etc. that I casually raised the question of the location of Gladstone's statue. This drew a blank with the PR officer. 'We've never had a statue of Lord Gladstone on the factory premises,' he declared. I pointed out that it was a historical fact that the girls had either sixpence or a shilling deducted from their wages, without their permission, towards the cost of the statue. It was because of what amounted to extortion that they turned the unveiling into a fiasco by pelting all the 'ladies an' gents' with eggs, flour and water. But despite careful scrutiny of the earliest ground plans there was no indication as to where the statue had been erected. Damn it all, you can't just lose a statue, and certainly not one of the dimensions described in the company's record books. As I searched the factory forecourt I was aware of the history that was here, the story which had become part of my own life. But no statue. Finally we gave up and went to lunch. The main topic of conversation was the missing Lord Gladstone and how the hell can you lose a statue? It was then I saw it, this giant of political history, now represented by a ten-to-fifteen foot piece of masonry. There he stood, magnificent above the ladies' lavatory in Bow Road, just by Bow Church. Was it just a matter of 'convenience' that the great man had been placed there? It couldn't have been symbolic of the Matchgirls' feelings ... or was it?

But this certainly was where the uproar at the unveiling

took place and where the statue has stood ever since. I think the original suggestion, as I recall, that the statue once stood in the factory grounds was nothing more than dramatic licence. More recently, just to check that the old boy was still there, I rang Bow Town Hall where a young cockney lass, all enthusiasm and dropped aitches said, 'Oh, 'e's still 'ere all right, right outside the ladies' lav, but someone's gorn and chucked a load of red paint over 'im!'

By the way, I had a reply from the Principal of the North-Western College of Speech and Drama, to whom I'd written offering my services, telling me their present curriculum didn't warrant another full-time lecturer. I sent him a couple of tickets for the London opening of *Matchgirls*, just in case there was a change in policy, but by then I was already involved filming *Georgie Girl* with Lynn Redgrave, James Mason and Alan Bates.

Then followed some more unexpected clutter. Leeds Music, a subsidiary of the Music Corporation of America, had bought the musical rights of *Matchgirls*, which made them responsible for the publishing of the musical score, sheet music, recordings and media 'plugs'. Most of that responsibility was borne by one of the directors, Don Agness. He was a very likeable guy who spoke my language and we became friends almost with our first meeting, prior to the show's London opening.

Our friendship continued after *Matchgirls* had folded, and we were having a drink in a pub off Charing Cross Road when, for no particular reason, I casually asked if lyric-writing was a closed shop in Tin Pan Alley. 'Not if you've got something to say,' he replied. 'Why, do you want to have a go?' I said I was certainly interested, so we finished our drinks and went back to his office where he gave me a recording of an Italian song called 'Pinnochio'. 'You're not bound to the Italian version,' he said. 'You're free to write whatever you wish.' I finally wrote nine lyrics to that tune, he turned them all down, but always gave a reason. However, with my second attempt at another Italian song, I wrote the lyric 'Marianne'. This time he accepted it without demur and Cliff Richard recorded it. My telephone began to ring to another tune, lauding another career. I've never had a big hit, but thanks to Don my catalogue was to provide another source of income. Seventy-five of my songs have been recorded by a variety of singers, including Al Martino, Engelbert Humperdinck, Sacha Distel, Matt Monroe, Caterina Valente, Jean Gabin, Frankie Vaughan and Ronnie Hilton. But when Don died my mentor had gone and with him my enthusiasm. I never wrote another commercial lyric from that day.

When I say I have never had a big hit, there were one or two near misses, and one of the nearest involved Sir Charles Chaplin. I had become the unofficial staff lyric writer for Leeds Music when one fine morning I received an urgent call from Don asking me to get along to his office at once. It seemed Charlie had premièred his latest film *The Countess of Hong Kong*, which had not been too well received by the press, and returned immediately to Switzerland where he became incommunicado. However, this was of no consequence to Leeds as the music publishers who had already arranged a couple of recording sessions for the one possible hit melody which eventually became 'Love Here is My Song'. I say eventually because Don, having booked the artistes, orchestra and arrangements, discovered only four days before recording that Charlie had left no lyric other than a couple of scribbled lines for the verse! All endeavours through Lady Chaplin to inform Charlie of the crisis had come to no avail. Almost in tears she lamented, 'He continues to walk around the garden pulling up my plants!' Now, whilst this undoubtedly gave us an interesting insight into the horticultural expertise of Sir Charlie, it went nowhere near solving the problem. So I was instructed to write, as Don said, 'as you would imagine this great man would have developed the lyric – from just the two lines he has already written'. The lines were:

Why is my heart so light,
Why are the stars so bright?

I have to admit to finding them uninspiring. But who was I to argue? I was going to share a contract with the world's greatest comedian! I wrote the lyric in Hyde Park, a stone's throw away from the office. I remember having doubts about one line of mine, 'Can there be too much love?' Too sophisticated, perhaps? Then suddenly an argument broke out between a man and a woman not twenty yards away. He slapped her across the face. I, like a typical Londoner, pretended it wasn't happening. Back to my muse: 'Can there be too much love?' – I decided to change it! The next morning I was told Charlie had finally been contacted and had made it crystal-clear that under no circumstances would he allow anyone else to write a lyric to his music.

Old cockney pro that he was, he phoned the completed lyric through within twenty-four hours. It became, I think, Harry Secombe's biggest seller, topping the three-quarters of a million mark. Within a few weeks Petula Clarke recorded it, selling over a million! But for me the music world did have compensations and acknowledgement in the years to come; one of these was being awarded by the Council of the British Academy of Songwriters, Composers and Authors their Golden Badge of Merit for 'service to British music'.

Round about now I began to pick up the strings of my political activities again. About this time the introduction of the Industrial Relations Act was heralded in and some of the bigger and more effective unions were beginning to flex their muscles. At that time, when membership of a trade union was regarded not with suspicion but as a democratic right, I remember ASTMS (Association of Scientific, Technical and Managerial Staffs) as being very active, led by their General Secretary, Clive Jenkins. They subsidized a short documentary film, for which all actors and technicians gave their services, of which I was one. With John Cleese I wrote a satirical cabaret for their annual conference which ended with everyone joining in a dance to the tune of the 'Hokey Cokey', but to a lyric I wrote, 'Oh, Crikey, it's a strikey!'

As I write this, I am reminded of a favourite TV play of mine, *Seventeen Percent Said Push Off* by Alan Plater, shown in May 1972, an excellent observation of 'caste', as the Victorians called it. The story centres around Gavin (brilliantly played by Robert Powell) who sets out to study the habits of the working class by temporarily living among them, staying with Dave (Malcolm Reynolds), who takes him around.

I played Dave's father, one who has given up on principles and, in consequence, just sits on the fence waiting for the inevitable. It was Gwyn Thomas, that master manipulator of words, who, in the *Western Mail*, so succinctly describes this character:

> ... TV at its most moving and mentally bright. The father is an extinct revolutionary who has long since shuffled away from his early barricade of burning dreams. In collarless shirt of flannel compromise, he drifts now down the Nile of Ale into an early dusk of resignation. Bob or two on the horses that are as infallible as old ideals ... Scared to lose. Scared to win, too.

Still politically active, I often meet old acquaintances from the past of 'burning dreams', so aptly depicted in the character of Dave's father, and who, in consequence, have become strangers to me. Occasionally during an interview the old conundrum is trotted out: 'Do you think your political views have hindered your career?' Before I answer I always make the point that I'm sure that such a question is never put to someone of my profession who is a known member of the Conservative Party. But I must say that I have never been aware of any such victimization. In any case, how would one know? If a management doesn't wish to employ me on political grounds, I guess that is their democratic right. Just let us be sure that we always have a government irrespective of politics, that will never allow a nightmare resembling that of McCarthyism to raise its ugly head in this country.

Working on *Matchgirls* with an apparently apolitical guy such as Tony Russell, it was inevitable that I found myself trying to explain the socio-political aspects of the period. I must say he was always attentive and genuinely interested. But on one occasion when offering some modern parallel to illustrate a point, he suddenly dismissed what I was trying to prove with the remark, 'Nothing matters, Bill.' Somewhat mystified, I asked him what he meant. He repeated, 'In the end, nothing really matters.' And with that I got the impression he didn't want to pursue the conversation any further, he wanted to get on with what we were doing. Because that mattered?

In 1969 Nina and I said farewell. She was not prepared to go on suffering and living with the ghosts of my previous marriage, a view with which I fully sympathized. We parted friends. In fact one year later when, in the small hours of the morning, she phoned, extremely distressed having just been told her boyfriend had been killed in a road accident, I immediately went to her. It would take a greater pen than mine to summarize here my relationship with Nina. Were too many highs followed by too many lows? We both tried, but she tried harder and kept trying until it all became too much. As a lover she was everything to me, no boundaries existed for her, she simply sought the unselfish pursuit of shared joy. And when I became ungrateful she walked away. As well she might. There had been much suffering in her life in the name of love, but she never would lose faith, she was a survivor.

Tom had left Lancing and as he was too young for Drama School, I subsidized him as a student actor at Leatherhead Theatre where he stayed until he attended an audition for a children's TV series, *Wreckers at Dead Eye*. He played a leading role, from which followed two other junior series,

Freewheelers and *Tottering Towers*. These were followed by several film parts, the best being in *Unman, Wittering and Zigo* and *Goodbye Mr Chips*. It was all happening, but it put paid to any ideas I had about an academic training for him. At the age of eighteen he was independent, shared a flat (rather tatty), owned his own car (very tatty) and was doing what he wanted to do. When I questioned him about it, he replied, 'What academic training did you have?'

It was in 1969 that I met Lindsay Anderson. I was being interviewed for a part in a new David Storey play, *In Celebration*, and Lindsay was to direct it at the Royal Court in Sloane Square. I remember him putting me at my ease on what was a very cold morning by discussing the merits of long underwear. Having got that out of the way, he then asked me to read from the play, which is the story of the Shaw family, including the father, an old Yorkshire miner, and I had to admit I had never played a Yorkshire part before. Some actors specialize in dialects, but I've always settled for giving an impression, picking key words, making the right sound.

Lindsay made no comment when I'd finished, he just thanked me and we said goodbye. I stood outside the Royal Court and somehow it seemed colder than when I went in. I was sure that was one audition I'd failed and I duly informed my agent. However, he phoned me the next day to tell me otherwise. Mr Anderson was offering me the part of Old Shaw, the Yorkshire miner.

This was to be the beginning of an association and friendship which lasted until his recent death. Our theatre work together, though sparse, includes three plays by David Storey – *In Celebration*, *The Contractor* and *The March on Russia* (retitled *Jubilee* for the tour in 1990) and they have provided me with three of the most effective roles of my career.

I was about to meet a company of actors none of whom I had met before: Constance Chapman played Mrs Shaw; Alan Bates, Brian Cox and Jimmy Bolam our sons, with Gabrielle

Drake and Fulton Mackay as family friends. Lindsay's original intention was to cast the play with Northern actors. However, he ended up with a very mixed bunch, but admitted after a week's rehearsal to feeling very confident. The play opened on 22 April 1969 to rave reviews for all concerned and I received my first fan letter from another actor! It came from Donald Sinden and I've kept it:

> My dear Bill,
> Very, very seldom is one privileged to see such a beautiful performance as yours in *In Celebration*. It is so much easier to portray evil than good – a 'bitchy' notice so much easier than a laudatory one. I sat there the other week at the Thursday matinée entranced by your beautiful observation of the father – good God! I've met him! I must have done! How many times have I seen *true goodness* portrayed? – Pierre Fresnay in *Monsieur Vincent*, Raimu in the *Fanny* trilogy; Richard Burton in *The Boy with the Cart* and Bill Owen *TWICE*. In this current play, and one in the war, or just afterwards, at the Theatre Royal, Brighton. But what was the name of the play? You were playing a very 'simple' youth! How do you do it? 10 out of 10, Mr Owen, straight to the top of my list of favourite actors. There are so many details I would love to mention, but if you are anything like me, you would never do them again, so I will just retain them glowing in my memory.
>
> Congratulations,
> Donald

The greatest thing for me about *In Celebration* was the feeling of being totally fulfilled as an actor, something I hadn't experienced in many years.

It had been a long time since the members of the 'Broken Marriages Club' had sat down to eat at the Grossmans', but it was there that Kathie and I met up again. Most of us had been involved at some time with Unity Theatre and naturally the conversation was one of nostalgia – the theatre was by now almost defunct – recollecting those halcyon days which were all we had to replace the beliefs, hopes and dreams of younger times. I was reminded, too, of the extent of Kathie's involvement in the initial stages of the *Matchgirls* musical. For love of the show, and also because I was short of the 'readies', she typed the first complete script. With only piano accompaniment she recorded all the songs with me, then when Tony Russell managed to get a small band together, she recruited a number of her friends to help with the singing.

All these years later, and in fact just five minutes ago, she brought me my coffee and, as usual, asked how things were going. I told her how I had been reminded of what she had done for *Matchgirls*, whereupon she reminded me that I forgot to arrange her audition for the part of Mrs Purkiss, a role she so wanted to play and for which she would have been perfect. Then as she left she also reminded me that I never sent her the two tickets for the opening night. And I *had* promised. I thought it best not to mention she'd forgotten the biscuits!

We've jogged along for over twenty years now, we don't gallop as often as we used to, but I'm a bit short of wind these days! Mind you, we went to the National Theatre to see Arthur Miller's play *After the Fall* which is purportedly an introspective of his marital experiences, including Marilyn Monroe. Was it a good play, you ask? Well, it was long! But as I said to Kathie as we left the theatre, on the basis of what we'd just seen, we were surely justified in announcing our silver wedding anniversary – when due of course. 'What paper were you thinking of,' she said, 'the *Melody Maker*?'

... Just a moment, she's back, *sans* biscuits but flourishing the *TV Times*.

'How's it going?'

'Fine.'

'There's an old movie of yours on the telly next week.'

'Go on – what's it called?'

'*The Comeback.*'

'It certainly has. Remind me to miss it.'

'You will, it's on Thursday at three o'clock – in the morning!'

'I'm not surprised.'

'Was it that bad?'

(I don't reply.)

'Do you want me to read the review?'

She beat me to it before I had a chance to say don't bother. 'The singer Jack Jones, funny girl Pamela Stephenson, comedy character star Bill Owen and urban hero Richard Johnson. One would have thought the chances of finding that quartet in the same film pretty slim. But in a horror film? The direction eschews all subtlety. The sobs and shrieks in the haunted house could only have come from Mr Jones' agent!'

10

Wine and Everything Coming up Roses

As I put Mr Shaw to rest, another of David Storey's father-figures emerged in the shape of a Mr Ewbank whose business is the hiring out of tents and marquees and who has a pivotal role in *The Contractor*. Whilst some may disagree with me that it is David's best work, I am certain it is his most observant. It is a play about labour from which there seems to be no satisfying end product. I quote here the last few lines of John Barber's excellent review in the *Daily Telegraph*: '... the result is an evening of slow, subcutaneous melancholy, a sharp-eared report on the casual infliction and the stoic endurance of suffering.'

The most charming and unexpected 'character' in the play is the marquee, slowly being erected by a team of five workmen, the employees of the surly contractor, Ewbank. Its crisp canvas awning gradually rises high and elegant on the stage and this is lined by a second tent, frilly in pink, white and green, equipped with a gleaming dance floor and decorated with bunting and hydrangeas. The prettier it gets, the more sour and ugly the workmen's conversation becomes. They josh one another at first, and then grumble and boast; a gang of drifters in a demeaning trade. Miserably poor already, the men begin to torment one another, but their boss Ewbank struts around, jingling his money, proud of the marquee being erected for his daughter's wedding. But he is unable to invoke the loyalty of his men or his son. A row blows up but comes to nothing. After the ceremony the marquee is dismantled, all the prettiness and all the ugliness have dissipated. Ewbank's family were played by Constance Chapman (wife), Judy Leibert (daughter), Martin Shaw (son), Billy Russell (father), Adele Strong (mother). His workmen, Philip Stone (Ray), Jim Norton (Marshall), T P McKenna (Fitzpatrick), Norman Jones (Bennett), John Antrobus (Glendenning). And I played Ewbank.

Lindsay Anderson's production was superb, able to co-ordinate all the manual layout with the careful unfolding of the scattered relationships which made it a touching and almost mesmeric evening in the theatre. I remember in particular one such moment which brought down the curtain on the first act. The marquee was complete in all its majesty, awaiting the celebrations of the next day. The men had gone home, the family had returned to the house, except for Ewbank himself who sat silent as though reflecting, on what? His failing relationships? His wife, his son, his daughter? Even on the ignorant bastards who worked for him? I willed the audience to try and understand my sorrow. The temptation was to indulge oneself, which would promptly bring a note from Lindsay (written on a postcard in red ink) reminding me of that fact. The play was transferred from the Royal Court to the Fortune Theatre, where it ran for almost a year.

Billy Russell and I almost worked together again in a series made by Yorkshire TV which had a political theme, with Colin Blakeley, Michael Gambon, and myself as the leading players. I say almost because at the first morning's rehearsal of the episode in which he was to appear, by a sheer quirk of fate I was to miss the most bizarre and shattering experience that could have happened to anyone. But let me explain. Billy was always early for rehearsal. During *The Contractor* he could be found sitting in the stalls at the Court, probably asleep, where he had been for at least a half-hour before anyone else arrived. So, on that first morning I also decided to get there early in order to have a chat before rehearsals began. As I climbed the stairs to the rehearsal room the Head of Drama for Yorkshire TV met me, and said, 'I wouldn't go in there, Bill. No doubt you're here early for the same reason as myself, to welcome Billy.' He then went on to describe how, when he arrived, he'd been met by a distressed young Assistant Stage Manager who told him how she'd made Billy a cup of tea, but when she took it to him he appeared to be asleep and she'd been unable to waken him. 'Actually,' he went on to say, 'I've just been in to examine him and I think he's dead.' I can only describe my reaction as being instantly numbed. If this man hadn't been here I would have gone up to the rehearsal room and Billy would have been, as I thought, asleep. I would have said to him, as I always did, 'Wake up, you old berk!' But he wouldn't have opened his eyes and replied, 'Oh, it's you, the other old berk!' Not this time.

Later in the day when things had more or less returned to normal – we had all been shaken by the experience – I asked the ASM if Billy had said anything to her. Apparently he had, but she didn't understand and rather than show her ignorance decided to make him a cup of tea, anyway. I asked if she could remember what he actually said, and she replied, 'When I asked him if he wanted anything to drink he smiled and said, "I'll have a gin and Domestos!" ' So he got a laugh as he made his final 'exit'!

The actor's instinct for scripts, to which I have already referred, was immediately alerted by a script that one morning's post brought me. 'Pilot script, *Last of the Summer Wine*, by Roy Clarke' read the first page. I began to read ...

EXT. SMOKY NORTHERN TOWN. DAY.
(Some stills to establish this (more Yorkshire stone than Coronation Street).

Beatles song Yesterday *being sung by Vera Lynn. Young girl walks down pre-war council estate carrying transistor radio from which the song is coming. She gets the fish eye*

*from three housewives in aprons and slippers gossiping at a
gate. The eldest (and hugest) one is Mrs Batty.*

*The girl and the song fade into distance. A small TV
retailer's van squeals to a stop outside Compo's gate. Driver
and youth go inside. Women watch from across the street.)*

MRS BATTY They're tekkin his telly again.
WOMAN God, is it Tuesday already?

EXT. COMPO'S HOUSE.
*(The garden's like a diseased head of hair. The door's open.
The driver and youth come out with the set. Compo follows –
pulling on his baggy old jacket. We see a great hole in his
pullover sleeve. He waves at the youth.)*

COMPO Does thee grandad know what kind a work tha's
       doing? So much for night school. *(He holds the gate
       for them.)*
          There's a step, sithee.
DRIVER We know there's a step.

(Compo watches them put the set in the van.)

COMPO Why don't you let me have one of them little
       portables? Save a lot of bother. Tha's going to be
       sweatin' when I get colour. And while tha's gorrit
       have a look at that vertical hold.

*(He watches them drive off – a lonely figure in the road tracing
patterns in the dust with the toe of his wellies. He walks over
to the women.)*

EXT. STREET. DAY.
YOUNGER WOMAN Mornin', Mister Simmonite.
COMPO Hey up love! I wish you'd stay inside, Mrs Batty –
       tha knows it only excites me.
MRS BATTY That's all he can talk. Filth.
COMPO But fluently. And your Harold's that wrapped up
       wi' his pigeons. Give us a word of encouragement,

Eunice, else stop flaunting thee laundry where I can see it. Washdays are purgatory. *(He starts walking away.)*

WOMAN No wonder his missis went off wi' that Pole.

(They watch him on his way. He pulls his old cap comforter out of his pocket and jams it on his head.)

YOUNGER WOMAN It's no fun being lonely.

MRS BATTY He's not lonely. There's a gang of 'em. Hang about that public library. They've nowt else to do.

YOUNGER WOMAN Poor old soul. What does he do when t' library's closed – wi'out his telly?

MRS BATTY Her next door says he exposes himself.

EXT. SMALL PRIVATE HOUSING ESTATE. DAY.
(The primly dressed (blazer with huge badge – service tie – pencil-line moustache) Blamire leads a beribboned tiny York-shire terrier. He looks with distaste at the scruffy urchin who appears and shows interest in the dog.)

KID Is it a pup?

BLAMIRE No it's not a pup. It's older than you.

KID Dunt it get troddon on?

BLAMIRE What do you want round here?

KID Can I gi' it a stroke?

(Blamire reluctantly and gingerly inspects the kid's hand first. The kid obligingly spits on it and wipes it down his trousers before bending to the dog.)

BLAMIRE You're a long way from home, aren't you?

KID No.

BLAMIRE *(anxiously)* You're not moving in round here, are you?

KID We're in. Next street. *(Blamire grits his teeth in a snarl.)* Me dad's gorra whippet. *(Blamire raises his eyes to heaven.)* An' a motor bike! *(Blamire covers his eyes.)*

BLAMIRE And two days' stubble on his chin. And sits out in
his vest. And a tattoo on his arm – go on.
KID A big dagger.

(Blamire winces.)

BLAMIRE Death or Glory?
KID Aye! Drippin' blood.
BLAMIRE Why aren't you at school?
KID I've got spots. *(Blamire yanks the dog away and wipes
the hand he touched the kid with.)* I'll be off then. *(He
goes off making cheerful farting noises ... turns round
and waves.)* See yer.

*(Blamire forces a sickly smile. When he turns away he sees
Compo.)*

BLAMIRE Oh my God, they're all coming through.
COMPO Mornin' Cyril.
BLAMIRE When I became a paying guest in this quiet little
backwater nobody said a word about it being in
the path of the migrating hordes of the proletariat.
COMPO What's up, Cyril?
BLAMIRE Let's have a bit less of the Cyril. Suppose the
neighbours hear.
COMPO Old schoolmates, aren't we?
BLAMIRE Shut up! *(He looks round.)* I'll deny it.
COMPO I saw where you were scarred once in the penalty
area. I can quote details, me owd love.
BLAMIRE Have less of the Cyril. I prefer the more rounded
tones of *Mister* Blamire.
COMPO Don't mind me telling you – but –
BLAMIRE Spoken respectfully while clutching your tatty hat.
COMPO Thee dog's crapping all over the pavement, you
know that, don't you?
BLAMIRE That's funny. He usually sews it up in little bags
and sends it by post.
COMPO Is tha frettin', Cyril?

BLAMIRE You don't have to call for me, you know. Suppose
I'm not going to the library?

COMPO Give over. She wain't let you back in the house till
teatime.

BLAMIRE Well she's not used to me under her feet all day.
You needn't think the only place I've got to go is
the library.

COMPO Tek this hairy pillock back home. Tha's dropped a
bollock there, Cyril – she's worse than a wife. Let's
go and meet Clegg.

(They walk on.)

BLAMIRE Five paces behind, if you don't mind, Simmonite.
I drag me way up by the boot heels out of Hardwick
Street and now – at the end of Life's Journey, here
you are again. Undermining me rising confidence.
There's not only me City and Guilds – there's this
social chasm between us.

COMPO Lend us a fag and I'll gi' thee a sniff at me socks.

A QUIET STREET

*(It goes uphill. Clegg (suit – cycle clips – boots – always a
clean collar and tie – comfy but clean check cap) is making
heavy weather of it on his old but serviceable bike, he is
further hampered by the bunch of wild flowers in his hand.*

*A funeral cortège overtakes him slowly. He tries to doff his
cap and wobbles precariously. He checks to see the street's
empty and sneaks a tow from the last car.)*

CHAPEL PORCH

(Vicar waits.

*Clegg props his bike and moves to the vicar's side. The
vicar looks at him warily.*

Clegg cups his hands.)

CLEGG This feller picks up this tiny bird in his hands – and carries its quivering little body across this busy junction and feeds it to his cat. *(Removes his cap. They watch the mourners follow the coffin through.)* Life's like that. A complex texture of conflicting moralities.

VICAR Agreed.

CLEGG So what are you doing here in your heavenly com- missionaire's suit?

VICAR Gasping for a smoke.

CLEGG Reckoning on you know what's on the other side.

VICAR Faith, Clegg. Faith. *(Clegg lights a fag. Taps the vicar's arm as he is about to go and offers him a drag.)* I'm supposed to be stopping. But then – it's hardly fitting for me to be seen trying to live for ever – is it. *(He takes a drag gratefully.)*

CLEGG I've finished the book.

VICAR You know where the others are. How are you keeping?

CLEGG Me bowels playing up a bit. *(He shrugs.)* God moves in mysterious ways.

(The vicar returns the fag and hurries after the funeral party. Clegg produces a pocket notebook and dons his glasses.
    Compo and Blamire approach Clegg who is making a note.)

BLAMIRE He's still calling for me in broad daylight. *(He points at Compo accusingly.)*

CLEGG Tell the neighbours he dunt belong to you. You're just looking after him for somebody.

COMPO They've tekken me telly again.

CLEGG Only because you haven't paid. It's nothing personal. *(He gives Compo the rest of the fag. Puts his book and glasses away.)*

COMPO What are you writing now?

CLEGG Just catching the passing thought.

BLAMIRE I don't know why you bother.

CLEGG Somebody's got to think about things. And who's
        got more time than we have? It's perishin' – let's
        move inside. *(He collects his flowers and bike and
        wheels it into the cemetery. The others follow.)*

At this point I put down the script, picked up the phone and
rang Jimmy Gilbert at the BBC to tell him I would be delighted
to accept the role of Compo in *Last of the Summer Wine* for
Comedy Playhouse. I had read enough to know this was
something unique in the annals of TV comedy. Mine was no
beginner's enthusiasm either, I'd recently been a victim of one
so-called 'laughter maker', called *Copper's End*, where Joan
Sims left the show after a disagreement, the police complained
that the scripts ridiculed the force, and the originator of the
series resigned after he saw the pilot! After that little episode,
Summer Wine read like gold!

At our first meeting with the author the three of us –
Michael Bates, Peter Sallis and me – expressed doubts about
the title of the show which we felt was too long and difficult
to remember. I heard a delightful variation on this theme when
one of our studio technicians told me about his mother-in-law
who, despite his constant explanations that *last* of the summer
wine was the title, still announced to all and sundry that,
'You'd better watch *Summer Wine* tonight 'cause it's the last
one!' It was twenty-two years ago when we trundled off to
Yorkshire for the pilot film location and I'm pretty sure that
the title presents no difficulty for our millions of viewers. But
there's always an exception, like the taxi driver last week who
said, ' 'Ere, 'ang on, you're in that *Port Wine*, ain't yer?'

The subject of the clothes we were to wear came up at that
meeting. We all finally agreed there should be one basic
costume for each character. Blamire (Michael Bates) in non-
descript suit, raincoat and trilby hat; Clegg (Peter Sallis) in
Peter's old demob suit, plastic mac and cap. Compo's costume
was discussed after lunch, during which the wine had flowed
freely. This may well account for the composite (forgive the

pun) and resulting impression of total dereliction which, during the first four series, I was able to perfect into one of the most identifiable costumes on British television.

And so it has remained for Clegg and Compo for the entire series, with the occasional lapses into sartorial excess by the scruffy one, whilst both Foggy (Brian Wilde) and Seymour (Michael Aldridge) have sought their individual limited variations. Looking at a photo of Compo taken during filming for Comedy Playhouse and comparing it with one taken a couple of years later, it's obvious that some changes have taken place. For instance, Compo started with a collar and tie! He wore a jacket without a blemish and a dark green, rather posh woolly hat, and there was no rope hanging down from his trousers! The sudden appearance of the rope is explained by the fact that in the earlier series I did most of my own stunts. In one particular episode I was required to climb the stone parapet of a railway bridge and walk across. During the climb my braces broke. Whether or not having my trousers round my ankles would have given the shot an added interest is hypothetical, the point is the director wanted my trousers as normal – well, as normal as Compo's trousers ever could be! – and *immediately*! It was a long shot, which means there would have been a delay whilst someone brought me a new pair of braces. I then remembered that among the many odd and unspeakable objects that Compo carried in his pockets was a piece of string. So my trousers were quickly secured and the shot promptly 'in the can'. But evidently the end of the string was clearly visible below my pullover, and the continuity girl insisted that it stay for the episode, by which time I had become rather attached to it. Later I had some window cord 'made to measure' and I've worn it ever since. The change of hat came about when an elderly lady in a fit of enthusiasm, or passion, knitted me three in a lighter shade of green, which I thought was happier for Compo, and I like the style, they sit on my head like a tea cosy. As for the jacket, that came about when the stunts became really dangerous and my double had to have an exact copy for himself and another should he lose it during a stunt. So three were made to measure, badly fitting, much to the horror of the tailor and then, when finished, were dirtied and torn!

The disappearance of collar and tie is down to my stepdaughter Kathleen Louise – known by all and sundry as 'KL'. She was going through that trendy period when it was considered chic to be seen wearing jodhpurs and tutu, particularly at a funeral. Oxfam were making a fortune! I can't remember what else she was wearing when she came to the flat one evening; all I could see was a tatty knitted silk scarf slung round her neck. A genuine piece of Edwardian working-class neck-wear worn like a tie around the neck but with each end tied to the braces, a mark of pride and caste and also convenient for throttling the rent man when he called. It was just what I needed, I had to have it – I demanded it! Without hesitation she took it from her neck and handed it to me, bless her heart. I had it made into four neck scarves, one I gave to a fellow actor, the others were worn by Compo – he's wearing the last now – and it won't hold out much longer!

Until it came to making the pilot for Comedy Playhouse, a visit to Yorkshire, as an actor, meant for me a week in Leeds, Bradford or Hull, cities I knew well by the early seventies. Such trips would of necessity include finding the best 'digs', the location of the theatre and the pub nearest to its stage door, and it was most unlikely that I would venture beyond these safe havens. So, travelling now along the highways and byways of the West Riding to find a suitable location was like journeying into the unknown. Five miles along from Huddersfield towards Holme Moss by the Old Manchester Road (great Catherine Cookson stuff, this) and we were in the valley of Holme ... then, suddenly, there it was – Holmfirth! A little town looking, I thought, rather 'down on its uppers' due, no doubt, to the fact that most of the mills in the valley were closed – the recession had been around a long time in Yorkshire. But it was a place with which I felt an immediate affinity. We used the Elephant and Castle at the end of Hollowgate as our location base and as I sat at the bar supping a half-pint, I had the growing feeling that I had been here before.

Twenty-odd years later that feeling of *déjà vu* has been transformed into one of *knowing* I am at home in Holmfirth and where I will no doubt find a final resting place.

Memories of the earlier series are, I'm afraid, somewhat vague. Quite clear in my mind, however, is the memory of one of the original members of our terrible trio, Blamire, played by the still much mourned Michael Bates. When we first met we were strangers as people and as actors, never having worked together before. But it is part of the thespian nature, on meeting for the first time, mentally to walk around one another, sizing each other up, as it were. Following that meeting, joined by Roy Clarke, we found ourselves thrown together in a pub-cum-hotel near Marsden in preparation for filming on location. Dinner time approached and we, now joined by Jimmy Gilbert, settled to drinks in the bar before going to our table. Cards were being played very close to our chests. There was much mild banter, lubricated with not so mild whiskys. Dinner followed, eaten with much good red wine. Suddenly, the most violent argument arose between Michael and me – politics, of course, and fuelled by the Nuits-Saint-Georges. Jimmy was trying to act as mediator, not too successfully, and not without a look of foreboding as he beheld two of his leading actors at it hammer and tongs even before a camera had rolled. But just as events seemed to be leading to a punch-up, Michael rose to his feet and said, 'Goodnight,' and went up to bed.

We never had a cross word again. We became good friends and, with our wives, shared many a social occasion. My friends will be amazed to have me admit that I'm not the most orderly and diplomatic participant in discussion, but it was Michael's bloody-minded and forthright refusal to come to terms or even consider my point of view that got me going. The following morning, about to start filming in a field with a herd of cows, we actors rehearsed and about to commence, I halted the proceedings with the question, 'Who's going to tread in the cowpat, then?' Michael immediately replied, 'I thought I would do that.' 'Good,' I said. 'As long as we know. OK, Jimmy?' Jimmy closed the subject with, 'Well, there's no point in the three of you doing it.' I believe that moment established a degree of professional honesty, trust and respect between the three leading actors which has been the basis for our successful ensemble playing.

It was after a pantomime rehearsal at Bromley that Dickie Henderson, also a friend of Michael's, and I visited him in hospital after an operation for cancer. I don't like visiting people in hospital, nor do I care for them calling on me, I just find conversation too difficult. But the inimitable Dickie, also gone, now, alas, rose to the occasion, putting us all at ease. We both attended Michael's memorial service, joining a congregation whose names read like *Who's Who in Show Business*.

11

Hooked on Holmfirth and Geese

Nowadays, a video is almost as vital a piece of equipment as the television itself, and no doubt totally taken for granted by my grandchildren William and James, but the fact is that when *Last of the Summer Wine* began no one had ever heard of such a thing. Even when they did appear I must admit to some reluctance in buying one. This was due entirely to my lack of affinity with anything mechanical, technical or, heaven forbid, computerized. I was in an electrical store recently and an elderly lady of Middle-European extraction was being instructed in the use of a word processor. Suddenly she stopped the assistant in mid-flow 'Ach, it's no use – they should give away a ten-year-old boy with every one of these!'

So you see why until recently, when the earlier episodes became available, the vast treasure of those adventures were forgotten or mere shadows as far as I was concerned. As are, and no doubt will remain, several of my TV drama appearances – Mr Zero in *The Adding Machine* by Elmer Rice, Charlie in *Passing Through* by David Ballentyne and, my favourite of all, *The Three Piece Suite* by Edna O'Brien. It is a splendidly written play concerning a doomed, illicit romance between a dull middle-aged couple, their half-articulated passion expressed in park shelters and along ugly river banks where, after experiencing their first kiss, the cloth-capped Romeo mutters, 'Your lips are chapped.' It was a play content to show people being just people, foolish, tender, greedy and drab. Directed by Quentine Lawrence, it was a joyful experience from beginning to end, particularly acting with dear Maureen Prior as Mrs Farley, my charlady 'femme fatale'!

Back to *Summer Wine*, though – being able now, thanks to the video, to view those early series I can see how the pattern of the relationships has changed. The stories for instance were almost entirely centred around the antics of first of all, Blamire, Compo and Clegg, but later other classic relationships were added.

The first I recall, at the beginning of the series, was that between a sex-mad librarian (Blake Butler) who was continually pulling his innocent female assistant (Rosemary Martin) down behind the counter where one assumed they 'stamped their cards' or he up-dated her catalogue! Marital relations have always been a serious subject in *Summer Wine*: journeys chartered on stormy seas of suspicion, non-communication and sex which, for the husbands, was lust for another woman, pigeons, the internal combustion engine, bachelordom, or to punch a certain bus conductress's ticket! For the wives, it was one of 'those things' to be endured, but at least it gave them a chance to look for any damp patches on the ceiling!

The two supreme examples were Sid and Ivy (John Comer and Jane Freeman) who, as they served tea and buns, hot pies and mushy peas, were likely suddenly to burst into a vehement argument regarding certain intimacies of their relationship, much to the amusement and interest of 'We Three'. The classic took place on the beach at Scarborough where we had all gathered, by coincidence or design, for a holiday. It was Roy Clarke at his brilliant best. The other rigid partnership was that of Nora and Wally (Kathie Staff and Joe Gladwin) though of a different nature. There was never any argument, just commands from Nora which Wally timorously obeyed, escaping when he could to the comfort and company of his pigeons. He would also gather a certain strength from his neighbour and friend, Compo Simmonite, who might brazenly suggest:

COMPO Don't forget, Wally, if tha' gets fed up with her, send her round to me, I'll have 'er.

NORA Are you going to stand there and let him talk like that about me?!

WALLY It's a fair offer, tha' could consider it!

Then, almost within a year of each other, John and Joe passed over, and suddenly there were two 'widows'. Whilst those hilarious picnic conversations with the motor bike can never be replaced, Nora at least has this scruffy would-be-Lothario living next door, who gloats through the curtain as she hangs her very large 'smalls' on the line. But I do think it's a pity that Ivy has not been paired off again, she has so much to offer – in every way! Think what she might do for Smiler!

Of course, one could say, depending on the circumstances, that the relationship between Compo and Nora Batty might be regarded as one of the classic love stories, vying with Romeo and Juliet, Antony and Cleopatra or even Michael Jackson and his missus. When Nora looks into Compo's bloodshot eyes something spiritual happens – his wellies steam up! 'Tis rumoured that he has to put them out at night and they have been seen strolling around the town on their own, with the Holmfirth Sanitary Inspector in hot pursuit. Like Richard Burton and Elizabeth Taylor they have been pursued by scandal and the tabloid press, hoping to catch them both as Compo grabs Nora by the bookmaker's and she wallops him with her handbag. Sensational headlines – 'Does Compo get his rompo?' Some blame must be laid at Terry Wogan's door when, over twenty years ago, he used to give daily reports on their derring-dos on his morning radio show.

But true love is still a rocky road – and Compo has the bruises to prove it. Nora wields a mean broom. The truth of it all is, of course, that it's all Compo's fantasy, just dreams in the head and certainly nothing below his non-existent belt!

Over the years new characters have been introduced with different relationships to explore. Edie (Thora Hird) and husband Wesley (Gordon Warmby) are probably among the nearest we cartoon characters come to the ideal marital solution. He almost permanently in his shed, clad in dirty overalls and she in her ever-sparkling kitchen – with plenty of newspaper on the floor! Then come Pearl (Juliette Kaplan) and husband Howard (Robert Fyffe) with Marina (Jean Ferguson), the scarlet woman lurking in the shadows, behind a wall, under a bridge or up a tree! Mind you, I'm sure if she were to take the initiative and reveal all to Howard he would disappear in a puff of smoke. This can only be described as the horror version of a *ménage à trois*! I think Edie's daughter Glenda (Sarah Thomas) has the right idea, she never expects too much of her husband Barry, with reason – for instance, I'm certain that if, having cooked the Sunday lunch, she sat down to eat wearing nothing but her wedding ring, his only reaction would be, 'Don't spill the gravy, luv, it's hot.'

It is surprising how coincidence has been responsible for introducing new faces to the *Summer Wine* team. For instance, Thora Hird happened to mention during an interview on television how much she enjoyed the programme. Alan Bell, our director, who happened to be watching, immediately enquired if she would care to make a guest appearance in an episode. She accepted and joined us for a full-length feature, *Uncle of the Bride*, playing Edie, and she's never left us! This was the film that also introduced Michael Aldridge as Seymour. Gordon Warmby had come down to be interviewed for a minor role in one episode, during which he assisted Alan to audition an actor for another by reading the part of Wesley and he gave such a good account of himself he became Edie's 'husband' and made his début in the episode 'Car and Garter'.

It was June 1984 and we were having a successful season of the stage version of *Summer Wine* at the end of the pier at Bournemouth. It had already proved itself a great success, both on tour and during a previous season at Eastbourne.

I must say, this being my first experience of summer season at the seaside, I found it a most enjoyable way to earn a living. At Bournemouth, for various reasons, certain characters had to be replaced, and Peter, Jane Freeman, Jean Ferguson and I were joined by newcomers Juliette Kaplan and Robert Fyffe. It just so happened that Roy had introduced three new characters into the *Summer Wine* series for that year, which we would begin filming on location in August. Owing to pressure of work he had not yet been able to see the stage version, so imagine our surprise when he and Alan paid us a visit at a matinée soon after our opening. The three characters – Marina, Pearl and Howard – were cast that afternoon. By now we were the flavour of the year, continually in the top-ten ratings and, with our Christmas show, topping *Gone With the Wind*!

We were wined and dined – the Café Royal, the Ritz, the Dorchester. One tabloid set up a stunt for Compo to have lunch at the Savoy, served in a luxurious suite, arriving by Rolls-Royce and making an entrance through the main foyer – startling one Arab gent and his many wives! I sat on an elephant with the Duke of Gloucester for Boys' Clubs! Nora Batty became the pin-up at certain establishments of high learning, and Compo opened summer fêtes and Christmas bazaars, even having his photo taken holding bonny babies. It was just like 1948 and the J Arthur Rank merry-go-round the second time around for me. *Summer Wine* was nominated for a BAFTA (British Academy of Film and Television Arts) Award. We won the Pye Radio and TV Industry Award and it was also voted by millions of younger viewers, through their TV show *Swap Shop*, as being the funniest television programme. Publicity was also coming from some unexpected quarters. The following is the text of a broadcast by the Rev. Bill Sergeant for BBC Radio 4 *Today*'s Thought for the Day.

Yesterday I was thinking about technological progress not always being the same as human progress – 'better' sometimes ending up as 'worse'. You can no doubt compile your own list from sliced bread to neutron bombs by way of self-suspending socks which fall in a heap around your ankles. Which leads me on to today's subject – Nora Batty and her stockings. Technologically, Nora is a bit of a mess, but humanly she turns Compo on – for him she is much better than sliced bread, better even than flying to the moon. If you haven't had the pleasure of meeting her and Compo then you should cancel all engagements on Monday evenings and tune in to BBC 1 and watch *Last of the Summer Wine*.

Three middle-aged men, all out of work, spend their time together in a Yorkshire village, ambling around, talking, thinking up ways of occupying themselves, getting into trouble, having fun. Compo (played by Bill Owen) lives next door to Nora Batty (Kathie Staff) – he frankly lusts after her. Why? For no obvious reason. She's married to Wally whose life she makes a misery – she nags him, browbeats him, tells him off. Why ever should Compo be attracted by Nora? Compo never takes his wellies off as far as we can make out – his socks smell! – he's invariably unshaven, he's never worked. Nora, not only in her better moments, despises Compo. But he loves her after his fashion. He's always manoeuvring her into situations where he can grab her and which end up with her hitting him with her constant companion, a broom – for Nora is as obsessively clean as Compo is incorrigibly scruffy. I think her attraction for Compo lies in her stockings. They wrinkle. They signal to Compo that she has difficulties in maintaining her superior standards – her stockings wrinkle like his socks smell. He is very ambivalent about this. Her stockings symbolize her likeness to the all-too-human Compo; but they also worry him because, to remain his fantasy woman, desirable but eternally beyond his reach, her stockings shouldn't wrinkle.

He buys her a frilly garter, and the opportunity comes when he can not only offer it, but when she can graciously accept it. He, disguised as a racing driver, a veritable knight, is for once socially acceptable. She, with unwrinkled stockings, is restored to ladylike (if not God-like) stature. But the car, exploding in clouds of steam and smoke, refuses to start – her stockings, despite the garter, concertina into wrinkles. So, by the grace of God working through the intractable nature of things, they are saved from their fantasies of super-humanity. They are not after all made of stainless steel and Teflon. They are Nora and Compo – in W H Auden's words, and I believe in the sight of God:

> Mortal, guilty, but to me
> The entirely beautiful.

And that's worth remembering as you look across the breakfast table.

As I had expected, with the growing popularity of *Summer Wine* offers of other television work became conspicuous by their absence. In fact, until February 1993 when, in company with Billie Whitelaw and Michael Gambon, we recorded for BBC TV *The Entertainer* by John Osborne, my last play for TV was in 1972, which was also the year of the birth of *Summer Wine*. Nevertheless, with the enormous popularity of *Summer Wine*, there came some surprising offers of work from the most unexpected quarters. For instance, I received in the post the manuscript of a musical show called *The Leyland Vehicles Road Show – All Singing and Dancing*. Let me hasten to add this did not refer to the vehicles, and the songs had not been written by Andrew Lloyd Webber! But singing and dancing there was with Les Girls and yours truly – Bill the hero! I don't remember much of the plot, if there was any. We did a few one-night stands before an audience of truck dealers who had been well wined and dined before the show, which lasted one hour, half of which was given over to a documentary film extolling the virtues of the Leyland truck. The mechanics of the show were such that they could only be accommodated in giant theatres like the Opera House, Black-pool or the Bristol Hippodrome. This was all summoned up in the finale when an enormous truck with me holding the steering wheel was navigated down towards the footlights by remote control. Never was there more combined praying by me and the musicians in the orchestra pit, willing the truck to stop when it should and, to everyone's relief, it did. Then I leapt out of the driver's cab and with Les Girls went into the final number. I can't remember what it was, maybe 'There'll always be a Leyland, whilst there's a country lane'. But when you're part of a show lasting thirty minutes which stars a truck, you take what you're given and smile! My bank manager did for several weeks, in fact he nearly bought me a drink!

When Sydney Lotterby, who has many successful credits in a long career with BBC comedy, took on the direction and production of *Summer Wine*, he asked me if I would be interested in helping with a video promotion. This was to be jointly made by ITV and the BBC with the idea of selling British comedy series in America, and Compo, he explained, was the only one required for the *Summer Wine* spot. I agreed and Sydney said they would be in touch. They were in due course and appeared to be very well organized, explaining that they simply wanted a shot of Compo riding around Nelson's Column on a bike; this would simply act as an opener to several excerpts from the series and would take no more than a half-hour of my time. I was given a date and the time a car would be at my disposal to take me to Trafalgar Square. I gathered from these details that this was going to be no small-time promotion, this was mid-winter and the obvious and cheapest way to take such a shot was on Sunday morning as soon as there was sufficient light, no traffic, no people. But no, they must have wanted plenty of action because they chose mid-week at 5.30 p.m. – right in the middle of rush hour!

On the appointed day, my costume was promptly delivered by BBC Wardrobe, and at the appointed hour a very large limousine was waiting to take me to Trafalgar Square. As we arrived, my feelings about this being no small-time promotion were confirmed – half of Trafalgar Square was illuminated by huge TV lights, hundreds of people were watching or milling about as the traffic became more frenzied.

The director met me, explaining that all he wanted was for me to cycle towards the camera which was a hundred yards away, and any 'funnies' I could think of 'would be more than welcome'. I remember I said, half jokingly, 'I suppose you've got permission from the police for this? but he was called away before he could answer. The first shot was OK for the director and me, but not the cameraman, so we shot it again and as I got nearer the camera I became aware of a policeman advancing out of the crowd. As he came towards me the thought suddenly flashed through my mind, 'I bet they haven't got permission to film here, the stupid bs'. The policeman interrupted, pushed back his helmet and said, 'Bill Owen, this is your life.' It was Eamonn Andrews.

I'm sure you must be acquainted with the format of the programme; a wonderful moment with my family – Kathie, KL, Tom, my daughter-in-law Mary and my grandsons, James and William; many friends, some unexpected like dear John Metzler who flew in from Florida and Freddy Davis from the Philippines where he had just collected a Gold Disc for a record he made of a song of mine, 'So Lucky'. A memorable evening!

In 1979 I returned to the National Theatre to rejoin Bill Brydon's company for his production of *The Long Voyage Home*, which comprised three early sea plays by Eugene O'Neill, to be staged at the Cottesloe. The title originated from a film version of the plays directed by John Ford, starring the young John Wayne, Barry Fitzgerald and Wilfrid Lawson. My introduction to the company had been two promenade productions adapted by Keith Dewhurst from Flora Thompson's book *Larkrise to Candleford*. This was my first experience of promenade theatre where the audience literally follows the action wherever it is taking place, in this instance spread over the entire floor of the Cottesloe Theatre. It can be very disconcerting at first, trying to act to a group of people almost eyeball to eyeball! Or pushing your way through a crowd of spectators in order to reach a scene before you start acting. I discovered there were two techniques, either you ignored the audience or you included them whilst making your way to a scene. I preferred the latter. For instance, in *Candleford* during a scene between Laura (Valerie Whittington) and Mrs Gubbins (Peggy Mount), which takes place in the Post Office, I, as Thomas Browne the postman, would have to pick my way through the audience, most of whom were by now seated on the floor. It was impossible to try and time an entrance, which often resulted in a pregnant pause as Laura and Mrs Gubbins waited patiently for me to arrive so that the scene could continue. I soon learned that a little improvisation to the seated audience was required, but still retaining the character and mood of the scene. So Mr Browne might say, 'You're gonna git a cold in your bum, you stay sittin' on that there grass,' or, to a man 'There were a stranger at the grocer's askin' for thee – she were pushin' a pram!' A few of those usually got me through in time!

Sydney Lotterby left *Summer Wine* in 1981 and was replaced by Alan J Bell, a remarkable man – well, he must be to have survived all these years in spite of us. Of course, he bears scars as proof, but his enthusiasm is never ending. I had a phone call from him this morning, from Yorkshire where he's charging about up hill and down dale looking for new film locations – but after twenty-three years there surely can't be any! But I would like to make it perfectly clear that you will never hear from me one word against my adopted county, just about the finest in the world. When Alan took over, a 'foreigner' from the South, as a form of introduction he kindly invited the three of us to lunch where I took the opportunity of giving him a friendly warning about the temperament of our occasionally fickle Yorkshire weather, which, like the people, comes generous and varied. For example, we might be up there on the moors waiting in the rain to film at eight o'clock in the morning and by four o'clock in the afternoon it's still bucketing down. So a demented film director, tears in his eyes, yells, 'All right, it's a wrap!' and everyone scampers back to the hotel to get out of their sodden clothes. But on the way, what happens? The sun comes out and we have a warm, balmy late afternoon and evening. 'If only we'd waited another ten minutes we might have been able to complete our day's schedule!' It's the voice of our by now hysterical director. If I seem to be adopting a know-all attitude it's because I happen to be an adopted Yorkshireman, a Fellow Member of the Yorkshire Society – to my knowledge the only 'foreigner' to receive the honour – and have therefore become well acquainted with our folk lore. You've never heard of the Pixie Tykes, or the old Ridings adage, 'Make magic on the moor and tha'll be wet, then poor'? What's film making but magic? And luck. My lips are sealed. I've said enough!

One of the finest summers we had enjoyed for a decade occurred in 1982, Alan's first year with us. Every day the sun simply shone and shone, we were ahead of schedule and he was able to indulge himself in some fancy camera work. Occasionally I caught his glance and with it a wry smile that seemed to say, 'OK, where's this weather, then?' The year 1982 may have been his introduction, but '83 was his baptism! The rain fell by the bucket, non-stop, well, that was until filming had been 'wrapped' for the day and the unit disappeared – then came the sun. 'Tis said that during one of these rainy days a film director was seen paddling across Cartworth Moor in a bathing costume raging at the sky – with two fingers outstretched.

Still in 1982, 6 June was the transmission date of an episode in the series *Tales of the Unexpected*, in which I appeared with Fulton Mackay and Harry H Corbett. It wasn't a very good story and one that, if I may make so bold, couldn't be made into a silk purse even by three experienced craftsmen. I knew Fulton of course, through *In Celebration*. Harry I'd never met before, but how well I remember his performance as the lieutenant of police in *The Power and the Glory*. He had played in a long and varied list of plays in repertory with Joan Littlewood at Stratford East, from which he emerged and became a leading actor in his own right and a household name with the popular TV series *Steptoe and Son*.

I looked forward to meeting him because I felt with my beginnings and experience at Unity Theatre we had some kind of bond, although Joan herself had no time for Unity. Whatever I expected from our first meeting however, I was disappointed. I can only describe it as cool, not that he was in any way unfriendly, just distant – as he was with everyone in the company. Throughout rehearsals he gave the impression of being in a hurry, with little patience for socializing. The director stopped the rehearsal in order to discuss a situation with us, from which Harry isolated himself, so the director turned to him for some comment, to which Harry replied, 'Can't we just get on with it?' which sounded almost like a plea.

We had one conversation together about pantomime and I told him of my only attempt to play 'Dame' and what a mistake it was. This was his last appearance on television and I think it was during his pantomime that he died. Fulton's words to the press were, 'Harry was under great pressure, both Bill and I felt it.' It was as if he knew time was running out.

In 1983 I was made an Honorary Member of the Associated Society of Locomotive Engineers and Firemen. Now, whilst this may appear of no particular significance, it was the first time that this trade union had conferred such an honour upon an actor. Politicians, visiting diplomats, foreign railway dignitaries but never before an actor! My association with this union began when Ray Buckton, the then General Secretary, commissioned me to present an entertainment as part of the ASLEF Centenary Celebration to take place before an invited audience at the Festival Hall in 1980.

The show was a great success, consisting of two parts, the first being a potted theatre documentary dealing with the history of the union in relation to the almost hysterical growth of the railway system, or variety of systems, that began competing with one another. The second part was an entertainment with several star names including Janet Brown who opened the proceedings as Margaret Thatcher and whose entrance not only brought the house down but angered one inebriated Glaswegian ex-shunter who, taking Janet for the real thing, announced to all and sundry, 'Ah'm nay stayin' here wi' that cow!' The speech that Harry Lovelock wrote for her was political, partisan and extremely funny; during it she continually referred to Ray Buckton as 'Mister Bunkup'. The music was supplied by the Grimethorpe Colliery Band who also recorded 'Centenary', a march specially written for the occasion by the American composer, Jim Cuomo.

Jim told me that in America there is no such 'animal' as an entirely brass band. All marching music includes reed instruments. So I arranged a visit to Grimethorpe where he would be able to sit in at a rehearsal and have any technical questions answered. The colliery now closed, was a few miles from Wakefield in Yorkshire and, like every pit village or town, it had its Miners Lodge to which, in Grimethorpe, the band's rehearsal room is attached. It was in there, packed like sardines, that I introduced Jim to the greatest brass band in the world – OK, so I'm biased! Introductions over, they snuffed their fags, the leader raised his baton and they began to play something by Mozart. I have never seen such an expression of wonderment and appreciation as I saw on young Jim's face as he listened. He then embarrassed everyone by applauding loudly when they'd finished! He told me on the train coming home it was a musical experience he would never forget.

*

As my association with Holmfirth, now christened the 'Summer Wine Town', has grown, I have purposefully gone out of my way to become involved with the community whenever I'm asked. Probably for the first time in my life I have wanted to belong. Saturday is our one day off when on film location, but not for me – I'm proud to say. I haven't had a free Saturday in years, there is always something going on somewhere in the valley at which my presence is required. I won't attempt to list all the organizations and activities to which my name is linked in that part of the West Riding for fear I should leave someone out. But I will mention the Saturday I marched with Neil Kinnock in a Yorkshire Miners' Gala and then was driven hell for leather back to Holmfirth to present prizes to the local Air Training Corps of which I am President. Sometimes a Jonah will ask, 'Do they appreciate it?' Ah, that's the question – or is it? Several years ago I was leading our torchlight procession through the valley when my eye caught a banner which read, 'BILL OWEN FOR MAYOR' – a joke, but I liked it!

As an actor my experience with animals can be summed up in one word – disastrous. In fact I have been forced to the conclusion that they just don't like me. For instance, I've been kicked by a horse, bitten by a falcon, trodden on by cows and I'm continually shat upon by ferrets, and please don't mention dogs! A further confrontation came about in a film called *Laughterhouse*, the story of a Suffolk farmer who, having fattened his geese ready for Christmas, is prevented from transporting them to Smithfield Market by an industrial dispute. Not to be outdone he decides to get them to London, as did his forebears, by walking them on their own two legs. In this film a lovable-looking canine, supposed to be my lifelong friend, behaved like a real pillock! Even when on a lead he wouldn't follow me. I was the one leading a dog's life. Eventually, Richard Eyre, our director, relieved me of this burden by sacking the dog for total incompetence. However, I did strike up a tolerable relationship with the geese, about five hundred of them.

In the story, such a feat of endurance captures the attention of the media, including a TV crew who follow them relentlessly, sending back daily reports to the viewers on the state and progress of their feathered friends. It is this growing popularity that is to give the final irony to the story. Having arrived at Smithfield where, thanks to their notoriety, the geese are unwelcome, I have to drive them in a hired truck to the slaughterhouse where I find the employees on strike, refusing to kill their TV favourites. It was a good cast, led by Ian Holm and Penelope Wilton as the farmer and his wife, with myself as the old drover. My only reservation was that I thought the script could have been funnier.

I have already explained the ending of the film, as it was seen in the cinema on its almost non-existent distribution. However, someone at Channel 4 had other ideas for the TV showing. Guess what? A happy ending! They cut the sequence of my final journey with the geese and the reception at the slaughterhouse. Instead it ended with Ian and Penny in a 'kiss and make up' scene – having been at each other's throats for the best part of the film. It ended with them walking away into the dawn, surrounded by carcasses of beef and a few sheep thrown in for good measure. They also changed the title to 'Singleton's Pluck'. Try saying that after a few large gins!

As for the geese themselves, I thought they behaved exceedingly well, not that I knew anything about the habits of geese when we started. Of course, I'm much more knowledgeable now and, I confess, a little shocked! It was the professional gooseman behind the scenes who, with a wave of his stick, could turn them round and have them back in position ready for a re-take in far less time than it would have taken to assemble five hundred human beings. By the end of the week, what with all that walking up and down on tarmac roads on their poor old feet (treated beforehand, as they did in the old days, with tar and then made to walk in sand) you would have thought the least that could have been done was to fit them all out with trainers! There was also the problem of harassment from the randy ganders, never knowing when you were going to be 'popped' one! But, come Monday, there they would be, all lined up on parade, looking like new. I asked the gooseman how he managed to get them so clean. He replied 'Daz.' But I don't remember ever seeing any with a blue rinse!

12

Tourist Invasion!

The 'discovering' of Holmfirth had begun with its inclusion in the official Yorkshire Guide Book as 'The Summer Wine Town'. Coachloads of fans were beginning to arrive, wandering around looking for the landmarks they had seen on TV. At that time once they had found Nora Batty's house and Compo's flat next door, then taken a walk to the church precinct for Sid's café, that was about it. Of course, if they were willing to risk the nooks and crannies, alleys and by-ways they might eventually find Clegg's front door – if lucky. There are only four cottages, not one of them numbered! But great fish and chips are to be had at Compo's café.

Whilst the structure and fabric of the town centre have remained unchanged down the century, since *Summer Wine* I have watched it slowly come alive again, picking itself up by its bootstraps and accepting the fact that it is famous and there's nothing anyone can do about it – only take advantage of it. Now Holmfirth boasts a new library, a first-class hotel, shops galore to satisfy every need and restaurants, pubs and a bistro to satisfy every taste. Bamforth's famous picture-postcard museum has a historic range including those of the 'saucy seaside' variety, which I can remember as a small boy – totally innocent of their innuendo, of course. Then there is the official 'Summer Wine Exhibition' with its extensive picture gallery and amazing array of original artefacts constructed expressly for the series, with mementoes for the visitors.

Through the busy, buzzing little town runs the river Holme, not wide, deep or rapid, but it is ours, with its sanctuaries of leafy glades, flowered walks and bankside picnic places – for which we must thank the Holmfirth Community Trust, a worthy team of volunteers who are concerned with the appearance and welcoming aspect of the town. There is a body of opinion, of course, that would wish us elsewhere, and their feelings have been expressed to me personally and to our director in no uncertain terms. Do they really wish to return to those days when we first arrived, when the river was a mess and changed colour according to what material was being dyed up at the mill at the end of Hollowgate?

Speaking of Hollowgate reminds me of one of my first encounters of an unforgettable kind when filming on the day of our arrival. I was passing a Chinese take-away where, standing at the door was the owner and his little son. I daresay neither of them had seen a film crew before and, showing off, I spoke, as a Tyke, to the tiny boy, 'Hey up lad, 'ow's tha' doin'?' The result was electric. The boy screamed and clung to his father's trouser leg, then they both hastily disappeared, slamming the shop door behind them, the father cursing me in what must have been his native tongue – I couldn't be sure, Chinese translators are thin on the ground in Holmfirth.

The Holmfirth Anthem
or
Pratty Flowers

Abroad for pleasure as I was a walking
It was one Summer, Summer's evening clear
There I beheld a most beautiful damsel
Lamenting for her Shepherd dear.

The dearest evening that ever I beheld thee
Ever, evermore with the lad I adore
Wilt thou go fight yon French and Spaniards?

Wilt thou leave me thus, my dear?

No more to yon green banks will I take thee
With pleasure for to rest thyself and view the lambs,
But I will take thee to yon green garden
Where the pratty, pratty flowers grow.

Now, before anyone takes me to task, let me add that I am
aware of the chorus that goes with our anthem, but this is as
printed in *Holmfirth from Forest to Township* by Eileen Williams and, either way, has been sung for over a hundred years,
crowning all convivial occasions when Holmfirth folk gather
together. I wonder how many times I have sung it through
the years? There was, for example, the Annual Torchlight
Procession which I led through the valley and down to the
field at Holmbridge where, after the prize-giving and fireworks
display, parents, children, elders and lovers sat in the flickering
light singing this, our own hymn, into the dark night. It is at
such times as these that I experience that wonderful feeling of
belonging that I mentioned earlier.

I have often been asked about Compo's personal safety, have
there ever been any accidents over the years with the risks he
so often takes? Now, whenever there's danger to life and limb,
a stuntman takes the risks, but let's face it, Compo will always
be at risk, he will never behave physically or mentally like an
old man of eighty years.
  Why, when walking on the pavement does he walk with
one foot in the gutter, why does he when walking the country
lanes choose the tops of drystone walls? Why is he always the
dupe for Foggy's crazy aspirations and ideas for furthering their
financial and social status? For example, careering downhill on
a pair of scooters (Yorkshire Remains), finding himself in
deep water (Wellies to Wet-suit) – and there was that really
dangerous caper when he wore a pair of large wings in an
attempt to fly, using the roof of a thirty-foot-high barn as
a launch-pad – in a gale! And he might have succeeded if it

hadn't been for three pairs of strong hands, off-camera, hanging on to his feet! I forget the title, I wish I could forget the episode.

The deep water incident involved Peter Sallis, Michael Bates and me. We were filming on the river, in a canoe. Fortunately we were wearing old-fashioned swimming costumes but I, like a fool, had kept my wellies on. Canoes are tricky craft to handle and in the hands of inexperienced amateurs such as ourselves the inevitable happened. It turned over. As might be expected, my wellies filled with water and I sank to the bottom. I managed to kick them off, but on my way to the surface passed Peter who was on his way down – a non-swimmer, I may add. Somehow I managed to get us both to the surface and as I looked around it seemed as if the entire film unit had jumped in to rescue us! Peter was taken off my hands at once, then a young man – one of the dressers, I later found – kept insisting on trying to rescue me until, finally, I had to tell him to piss off, explaining I was more than capable of saving myself. Later I realized I had been more than ungrateful and exceedingly rude. I apologized but he was very uptight with me for the rest of the week!

The longing for Nora Batty is just a fantasy, all in the head and certainly not below the navel. Compo was offered the opportunity of bed when he advertised for a housekeeper. There she was, willing and waiting and what did he do? Blew 'Come to the cookhouse door, boys' on a trumpet! How bizarre can you get? The secret of Compo is that his life is still controlled by impulse, each day is lived on the spur of the moment. He has never really grown up, at heart he is still a boy ... 'Me grannie were workin' in't mill when she were eight year old, she told us 'erself when I were a kid, everybody 'ad to work at mill in them days, if they didn't they starved, or went poachin'. That were all reet if tha didn't get caught, but if one o' them keepers caught thee tha bore scars to tha dyin' day. Story goes me grannie were jumped by foreman one time when she 'ad to bring samples to 'is office like. She were only sixteen and there she were wi' one up the spout! She were sacked from t'mill and 'er father threw 'er out, so she went 'ousekeepin' for two of 'er cousins, them what 'ad a small farm up 'ere.'

'Up 'ere' happened to be Cartworth Moor; 19 June 1992, the date of this 'conversation' which was the twenty-first anniversary of our first arrival in Holmfirth for the filming of the pilot of *Last of the Summer Wine*. It was a beautiful day and I had decided on a lunchtime picnic – alone. I wanted to think about this momentous happening in my life – that was when 'he' joined me.

So in the warm haze of that glorious location, no doubt aided by a couple of glasses of ice-cold Chablis, we 'talked' for the first and only time. I asked him if the two cousins accepted the fact that his grannie was pregnant? . . . 'Oh aye, they would probably never 'ave bothered, after all she were sharin' both their beds.' 'Your grannie must have been a glutton for punishment,' I said. 'No, that went wi' the job of 'ousekeeper in them days and she 'ad a job for life as long as she behaved 'erself.' 'And did she?' I enquired. 'Ay, she saw both o' them to the grave and inherited the farm, such as it were, but me mam were safe and grew up wi' a roof over 'er 'ead, that were till she met me dad.' By now he was at his usual pastime of plaiting stalks of grass together. I asked him what his father was by trade. 'A tinker, when 'e weren't in t'nick.' Pressing the subject I asked how often that was. 'More often than when 'e were at 'ome,' he replied, then continued. ''E 'ad a reet likin' for church rooves. But if 'e come 'ome drunk, me mam would belt 'im then put 'im abed and tha'd not 'ear another squeak outa 'im until opening time. Me mam, she were as tough as old boots, she 'ad to be rearin' a brood o' seven lassies an' me. I was 'er favourite, she'd take me on t'cart when she went round sellin' clothes pegs and collecting scrap. I loved me mam. It was only Alice an' me that went to school like . . .'

I halted his flow of reminiscences with the offer of some

Chablis which he drank in one gulp, followed by the remark, 'Gnat's piss!' Ignoring the insult, I asked him about the village school. He nodded, 'It served several villages, but tha' 'ad to 'ave boots. Cleggy's father were 'ousepainter, but it were Foggy that'd come to school as clean as a new pin, 'e 'ad a crease, can tha' believe, in his short trousers. But when it came to goin' 'ome, oh dear...'

This brought to mind probably my favourite scene in the whole twenty-odd years of the series.

The scene is the bridge at Hinchcliffe Mill where Clegg and Foggy sit feeding the ducks, waiting for Compo who is under the bridge trying to get into a wet-suit which he's just bought off Sid for a fiver which he borrowed from Foggy. It is very peaceful.

CLEGG Do you think he'll be all right under the water?
FOGGY I think it will be a great improvement.
CLEGG But will it be safe?
FOGGY I have every confidence.
CLEGG In *him?*
FOGGY No, how could anyone have confidence in him? No, I mean I have confidence in our ability to fish him out if he gets into difficulties. (*Calls to Compo*) Are you coming?
COMPO (*off*) In a minute! It's not all that easy getting into a wet-suit.
FOGGY I hope you're not putting it on over your wellies.
CLEGG It gives you a funny feeling when you know a fellow you went to school with has grown up into somebody taking his clothes off under a bridge.
FOGGY He was weird even at school.
CLEGG Only from nine till four.
FOGGY When I remember him and Twiggy Hopwood, they must have stuffed hundreds of beetles down my trousers.
CLEGG Only one at a time.

FOGGY Exactly. It was a monotonous regularity. 'Hey up, here comes Dewhurst!' Bang! Wallop! A beetle down your trousers. No it was my mother I felt sorry for.

CLEGG Why?

FOGGY Well, she used to go round with that tight expression. I know she hated the idea but she was trying to come to terms with it.

CLEGG What idea?

FOGGY Well, when you've been her only child she had nothing else to go by, and she was beginning to suspect that it was normal for a growing lad to go about with beetles in his trousers. She used to brush my hair last thing at night and I'd be standing there, all shining, you know, nice clean pyjamas, and I remember she used to look at me with a deeply disappointed expression every time she passed me my Horlicks. Nothing with her sheltered upbringing had prepared her for a growing lad with beetles in his trousers.

CLEGG But couldn't you remove them at school, it wasn't compulsory to bring them home.

FOGGY You couldn't always find the time or privacy. No, it wasn't the sort of operation you could pull off in a public place.

CLEGG Yes, I can see that.

FOGGY And you remember what school teachers used to be like in the early thirties.

CLEGG They nearly all had little moustaches, and I don't just mean the ladies.

FOGGY Imagine being caught by one of the old school fishing about down a pair of trousers.

CLEGG Especially your own trousers.

FOGGY Yes, try telling one of them you were only looking for a beetle.

COMPO (*off*) I'm ready now! Is it all right to show meself?

FOGGY Well, you've been doing it without anyone's permission for years, why bother now?

COMPO (*off*) Here I come!

(*Compo appears looking like a rubber duck.*)

Get a few actors together, bring up the subject of theatre ghosts and you can be sure you're in for a long session. Three immediately spring to mind where they are said to glide the boards: The Opera House, Buxton; Theatre Royal, Bath, and the Royal Court, Sloane Square. Many more have their ghosts, and the stories get taller and taller as the hour grows later and the drinks come faster! I've been told that a butterfly in a theatre is the ghost of an actress. Well, I can't vouch for its sex, but we did have an odd experience with a butterfly when Peter and I were playing a summer season at the Devonshire Park Theatre in Eastbourne with the stage version of *Summer Wine*. One evening after we had been running a couple of weeks, a butterfly flew on to the stage and immediately captured the audience's attention by fluttering gracefully whenever anyone began to speak. We tried to make a joke or two, like 'Don't worry, it's got an Equity card', but when this developed into a nightly appearance, including kamikaze attacks from the chandelier, our patience became a trifle short. Then, as suddenly as it had arrived, it disappeared ... That is, until our final performance of the season when, almost at the same spot in the play that it had made its original entrance, it made another and, as the audience laughed, we groaned.

But our worst fears were relieved when it just flew twice around the scenery and left the stage to a burst of applause. At the end of the play when the curtain rose for the company to take their bow, it reappeared and settled in the middle of Compo's woolly hat, just above my nose, and there it stayed as we took bow after bow and, as the curtain fell for the last time 'she' flew away. The ghost had gone. The other members of the company there – Jane Freeman, Liz Elvin, Jean Ferguson, Ken Waller, and Peter – will confirm this story.

For me, one of the great events of the seventies was the filming of the play *In Celebration*. Lindsay Anderson was to direct, and it was his decision to wait until his original stage cast were all free to play their old roles in the film. This was in spite of suggestions from the production company, American Film Theater, that perhaps more important names be sought, such as Laurence Olivier, who might consider playing Shaw. But I'm told Lindsay was adamant. This, the American Film Theater's second season, covered a broad canvas of subjects which their publicity blurb pointed out were '... not mere images of the play, but film with all the technical qualities and all the magic that only film can create'. They had some big names. Joseph Losey directing Topol and John Gielgud in Brecht's *Galileo*, Maximilian Schell in *The Man in the Glass Booth*, Glenda Jackson, Susannah York and Vivienne Merchant in *The Maids* by Genet, directed by Christòpher Miles, and last, but certainly not least, *In Celebration* by David Storey, directed by Lindsay Anderson, starring Alan Bates and the rest of the original London cast, with the exception of Fulton Mackay.

The American Film Theater was a bold and innovative idea in the art of film making and would, I suspect, be laughed out of every accountant producer's boardroom today from here to Tokyo. Nevertheless, their bankruptcy, which I'm told occurred after the second season, was due to the simple fact that their business acumen did not match up to their artistic endeavour -- and that spells disaster in any language.

But it was great being back with the Shaw family again: Constance Chapman, Alan Bates, Jimmy Bolam and Brian Cox as 'my wife' and three sons, with Gabrielle Drake as our neighbour. The character of Reardon, originally played by Fulton Mackay, was taken out of the film script for some reason. With the film's almost non-existent release in Britain in 1975, I was asked to make a personal appearance in Nottingham. It was a Sunday matinée, the cinema was almost full and as I walked out on to the stage all the razzmatazz of twenty-five years ago came flooding back. Bill Owen – J Arthur Rank star! Personal appearances here, there and everywhere! ... a few jokes, an impression or two, a song ... I'd have 'em eating out of my hand! But not that Sunday afternoon, no clowning. I just talked about the film for a few minutes, then bid them goodbye, confident that I was leaving them with the greatest film performance of my life.

It seems there was always talk about filming the musical *Matchgirls*. I can remember having a conversation with an American producer whilst we were still in rehearsal. Director Ken Hughes showed great interest, and it continued long after the show came off in London. There were certainly three production companies who, each in turn, proclaimed serious intentions. I was invited to production meetings where discussions took place involving casting, directors and budgets. There were some results from one of the production companies: Gene Kelly agreed to direct the film; Lindsay Anderson would work with me on the film script; we'd have Vanessa Redgrave as Annie Besant, subject to script, and Barbra Streisand as Kate? (It was hoped Gene Kelly might persuade her.) And Howard Keel as Joe – to be sent a script. But there was one thing they never told me – where the money was coming from! Not long ago – all these years after the musical was produced – I heard again from this 'producer', but a few small points worried me – as when he told me he was telephoning from a friend's house as he couldn't pay his phone bill.

Another interested producer, Stanley Dubens, took me on a tour of the idle London docks and I became very excited at the prospect of using them as a location. During our tour we were stopped by a policeman who wanted to know what we were doing on private property. Stanley informed him we had permission and I explained the purpose of our presence, which seemed to capture his interest immediately. He explained that he was of the fourth or fifth generation connected with the docks and had started work as a docker. He knew the story of the Matchgirls – it was history in dockland – and he also regaled us with information about the dockers' lives, their practices, and their poverty, the like of which I had not come across in any of my research. I took notes.

There is one story of his that I shall always remember. Dockers were casual labour and had to present themselves every morning, very early, at the dock gates where they were huddled into an iron cage. The foreman would then appear and parade up and down outside, handing out work tags. If he got bored he might toss all the tags over the top of the cage and let the men fight for them – like animals. A hazard the foreman had to be aware of when handing out the tags to the hands stretching out from the cage was the likelihood of a man, out of sheer desperation for work, spiking the foreman's wrist with a large meat hook, snatching the tag and disappearing into the crowd. His mates remained silent; they'd seen nothing!

That was many years ago and all the good intentions about a film of *Matchgirls* have faded along with the notes I took from that policeman at the docks, and I never did have the pleasure of hearing Howard Keel sing songs from *Matchgirls*. But we did warble on another show; no, not as a duet, but in the TV production of *Kiss Me Kate* by Cole Porter, directed by James Gilbert, to mark the opening of BBC 2 in 1964. Patricia Morrison and Howard Keel were brought over from the States to play Kate and Petruchio, roles they were both well acquainted with, whilst our own Millicent Martin and Irving Davies played Bianca and Lucentio. Danny Green and I played the 'Gangsters', characters unknown to the Bard but the invention of Cole Porter who wrote 'our' great number, 'Brush up your Shakespeare'. What a show! What music! What songs! And the performers were pretty good, too!

13

Friends and Memories

I'm often asked to explain the secret of *Summer Wine*'s success. There's no short answer to that one. How *does* an unsophisticated television comedy with plots and characters invariably 'over the top' regularly hold a place in the Top Ten ratings, with viewing figures of eleven million, young and old, continue indefatigably towards not just being an institution, but a cult, and one which the BBC have (unsurprisingly, maybe) never given any indication of withdrawing? Just what are the ingredients required to have children write in asking if I can have a word with their parents about allowing them to stay up late to see the show? Or the grandparents who told me their grandson had been in a coma for months and as *Summer Wine* was his favourite programme, would I, as Compo, make a tape they could play at his bedside to see if it would help him back to consciousness? Some months later they wrote to tell me he had in fact done so. And then there was the lady from New Zealand where, apparently, the series is very popular, who stopped me in Holmfirth where she was spending her holiday in 'Summer Wine Town' and asked if I would send a signed photograph of Compo to her friend back home who had cancer. So a photograph of this outrageous little clown, dressed like a scarecrow and grinning like a garden gnome was duly dispatched to Mrs Gubb in Auckland, New Zealand.

I did hear from her and I hope she won't mind if I quote part of her letter: 'Not once since the diagnosis have I shed a tear, but when I opened your envelope the tears ran down my face. It was so very kind of you to take the time to comfort me in such a way.' Throughout the letter she refers to me as 'my Compo'.

Talking of the power of television brings to mind an occasion, before *Summer Wine* and during my popularity as a panel game host, when young Tommy and I were walking home after a fishing expedition off Brighton Pier. A man came up to me and said, 'I know you, you're in that television game, ain't yer?'

'Yes, *Keep it in the Family*.'

'That's it! Bill Owen – good, never miss it.'

'Good.' A long pause.

'You know me, don't you?'

'I have never met you in my life.'

'But you *must* know me ... I see you every Wednesday!'

The humour in *Summer Wine* is in the tradition of Charlie Chaplin and Buster Keaton; it has neither pretension nor embarrassment and, regardless of plausibility, maintains its integrity. Combine these values with a cast of excellent players, mix and stir well into the incomparable beauty of the West Riding and you've got a right good summer pudding – or, as in our case, a great Summer Wine ... that travels!

Loath to tear myself away from the subject of that glorious countryside, I have to mention one spot in particular, a favourite of mine and our director Alan Bell's. It's called Intake Lane and it eventually saunters to a crossroads that then seems to give up the ghost, I suppose because it's so high up there's really nowhere else to go. Standing there on a warm summer's day, waiting for the others to arrive, eardrums bursting with the silence, I'm faced with a panorama that never ceases to arouse in me the wonder of this planet, despite our greed and determination to destroy it.

I have a theory that I can only describe as evolutionary, concerning the changing attitude to old age and it takes me back to a train journey to Yorkshire and the ticket collector, who would not be collecting for much longer, and was looking forward to waking his spouse with the question, 'Right, gel, what shall we do today?'

Nothing about retiring, lazing in rocking chairs or resigning oneself to the inevitable but 'Today's a fresh start!'. A new adventure – that is, of course, if one has a realistic pension. The whole concept of ageing has changed now we are living longer. In fact I have read that in the not too distant future the senior citizens of this world will exceed the rest of the population. Going back over twenty years to the pilot script of *Summer Wine*, it is basically the story of three senior citizens faced with the challenge of living for the day, simply getting on with life. Now, whether the author was consciously pre-empting these changing attitudes, I have never asked. But, nevertheless, I am of the opinion that it was the unique spirit and bravura of these geriatric 'Just Williams' coming at such a time which gave it its own longevity and made it totally acceptable. I said there was no short answer – but it is my own.

I've done my best to analyse the relationships between the other characters in *Summer Wine*, that is with the exception of Eli – and who would dare attempt an analysis of Eli, particularly when he's down at The White Horse ready to play darts! As for Foggy, Clegg and Compo, I think their relationship has been more than amply illustrated down the years, despite the fact that Foggy sought pastures new for five years to be replaced by Edie's brother, Seymour. Poor old Seymour, the failed schoolmaster and inventor. The only man to make Heath Robinson appear uncomplicated!

But the recurrent and I suppose inevitable question I'm asked is regarding our personal relationships, Brian Wilde (Foggy), Peter Sallis (Clegg) and Bill Owen – the actors. There are still busybodies who quite casually ask how we get along after all these years, hoping, of course, to see me tear my hair out and reply, 'We hate the bloody sight of each other!' So they are usually abashed when I reply, just as casually, 'Oh, we get along.' This can be a red rag to the really persistent ones who then say, 'Oh, come on, you're not going to tell me you don't have rows or disagreements, that there's no jealousy!' Nonchalantly I murmur, 'Very rarely.' But if they continue to persist I confront them, eyeball to eyeball with, 'Have you ever heard of Duke Ellington?' Stepping back, they give a puzzled nod and I relate the story of the great maestro being asked, 'How have you managed to keep a band of such talented musicians together for nearly forty years?' He simply replied, 'Money.' An oversimplification, of course, and it doesn't quite fit the bill as far as I'm concerned. For me *Summer Wine* has become a way of life and one I find difficult to contemplate being without. But money does come into it, an important factor for the three of us, particularly over the last ten years or so. And it would be hypocritical to pretend otherwise.

Before leaving the personal relationship issue, I'd like to say that Peter's and mine has been the most consistent since the series began, and during that time we, as characters, have had to adjust and re-adjust to the changes fresh characters have brought about as they have come and gone. I would claim that as actors we have brought the relationship between our two characters to a fine art, our timing and reaction during one of those now rare moments when we are alone together is still a joy to me. But outside our shared love of classical music, about which Peter has enlightened me and broadened my knowledge, I think we have very little in common. Even less I feel with Brian Wilde, whom I've always found to be an extremely private person. In fact I believe my whole concept of living is different from theirs. For instance, and I speak from experience, the subject of politics is taboo, not from any strong opposing views on their part, but simply because they appear to be apolitical. They cannot understand how I can possibly give up my day off to get involved with the local community of Holmfirth. We have a caravan the size of a self-contained flat in which we have each reserved a corner to enjoy our own privacy which is strictly observed. We rarely communicate between series, meeting the following year for the first time at a script conference prior to going on location. But, like I said, 'We get along.'

I am reminded by a photograph of myself and the Mayor of Camden unveiling a plaque to Unity Theatre on 1 April 1992, which marked the dates of its beginning and its end. The end came in the early hours of 5 November 1975, when Unity Theatre was destroyed by fire. The only habitable part of the building that remained was a room over what was left of the coffee bar. There were various rumours as to the culprits – the local National Front, vandals, and even children (which seems highly unlikely at four o'clock in the morning). On that day I was at the Annual General Meeting of our union, Actors' Equity, completely unaware of what had happened until the president, Hugh Manning, announced prior to the beginning of the meeting that Unity Theatre had been destroyed by fire in the early hours of the morning. I sat stunned. Although the theatre had by then become barely a shadow of its former self, and I had had little or no association with it for many years, nevertheless it was a shock. A year or so later I was asked to attend a concert given on behalf of the New Unity Theatre Building Fund. Reluctantly I agreed, but asking myself, Why bother? There were professional groups now doing the job Unity should have done. Was this going to be just a trip down memory lane? If so, where were the beliefs, where was the commitment? Enthusiasm such as ours was born of a bygone age and could never be recaptured. However, in spite of my protestations, when Alfie Bass, actor and lifelong member of the Theatre asked me to become a member of the Unity Theatre Trust, I agreed. I must admit to being somewhat surprised and apprehensive when I received notice of my first Trust meeting and discovered it was to be held in the one habitable room attached to the burnt-out building. It was very strange in the evening half-light, walking up the path to the theatre forecourt after all these years and then, suddenly, there it was, just as I'd always remembered it, the front of the building almost untouched. But the truth was yet to come.

When the meeting was over, someone suggested that I might care to see what was left of the theatre. Given the courage, I should have refused. What morbid interest was there for me in the four blackened walls with only the night sky for a roof? Except a thousand haunting memories.

Before slipping the photo of the unveiling back into its cover, let me explain that the occasion was also part of the opening ceremony of Unity Court, so named in further homage to the theatre. It consists of several private dwellings and accommodation for the elderly and families in need. It was a very emotional time for those of us who remembered the glorious years when that little converted chapel became a shrine to the radical awakening of so many of its innocent congregation. Now, truly Phoenix-like, it had risen from its ashes to become a permanent, living memory.

A while ago I was invited to a gathering for the official launching of a new publication, *Sixty Voices* by Brian Mc-Farlane of the English Department of Monash University, Melbourne, Australia. The work was a collection of sixty interviews with various actors and directors prominent during those boom years of the British Film Industry between the forties and the early seventies. Looking through the list I recognized the contributors, most of whom had had their moments of glory, with their names emblazoned across the hoardings of the local cinemas during those golden years when a queue outside a cinema was taken as a matter of course. The days when a cinema was alive with usherettes, and a resplendently uniformed doorman – usually an ex-NCO and looking the part – stood guard over his domain and eagerly waiting charges, exclaiming, 'Ai've two singles at one and nane.' That was the moment when, if you wished to impress your new girlfriend you whisked her out of the 'one-and-nane-penny' queue and marched her past the peanuts and up to the box office – with maybe a white-gloved salute from the doorman – to splash out on the two-and-threepenny seats.

There are some of us of course that are still around and working or waiting, others who are known to have retired and some who it would seem have just faded away. This often leads, particularly among elderly actors like myself, to the inevitable question, 'I wonder what happened to ...?' But I hasten to add that when such a question arises, I not only refuse to participate in the ensuing gossip but I also leave such company. The reason for this apparent rudeness lies in a television interview I gave many years ago when I was reminiscing about theatrical landladies and I quoted a hilarious experience told to me by Garry Marsh, an actor I had been with in the film *Dancing with Crime* and to whom I naturally gave credit for the story. It was then that the interviewer interrupted me with, 'Whatever happened to Garry Marsh?' to which I replied with total conviction, 'I regret to say he is no longer with us.' The next morning I received a letter which ran, 'Dear Bill, Sorry to disappoint you, Garry'! I had announced to millions of viewers, including his family, friends, agents and the entire acting profession that he was dead, when he was actually alive and kicking! Of course, I sent my abject apologies not only to him but to every showbiz journal. Fortunately, there were no further repercussions, but I did develop the habit for a while of looking over my shoulder when leaving my house.

There is a less dramatic and perfectly logical reason why some actors seem to fade away, this was given to me a couple of years ago when I was at the Royal National Theatre with the play *The March on Russia*. One evening after the performance I was visited by Rosamund John, a very popular filmstar during those boom years, and during the conversation I asked her why she didn't act any more. 'Because no one asks me,' was the reply.

But back to Mr McFarlane's *Sixty Voices* in which I also featured. At long last, I thought, a complete list of my film credits! But no, even I could recall a couple of titles not listed – remembered, I must confess, *after* the book had gone to print!

Some of these long-forgotten films do still crop up from time to time. Kathie has just appeared with a cup of tea and informed me that she has been watching me perform in an afternoon film on TV called *The Hellfire Club*.

'That rings a bell. What was it about?'

'You were very physical, sword-fighting and jumping about all over the place.'

'You mean like Errol Flynn?'

'Not quite.'

'Did you record it?'

'No, I didn't think you'd want to bother with that sort of thing.'

She took my empty cup and retired – I got my biscuit this time!

But what did she mean 'bother with that sort of thing'? Bother with what sort of thing? So I looked it up in *Halliwell's Filmgoer's Companion*, an invaluable reference book for old films, including those best forgotten! *The Hellfire Club*, released in 1961, had starred Keith Michell, Adrienne Corri, Peter Cushing and myself. It all came back to me, I played Keith Michell's friend and partner in a circus act who accompanies him when he returns to claim his rightful inheritance, which at one point in the story necessitates our confronting the Hellfire Club in their cave, during one of their orgies. Now I see what Kathie meant – I *am* too old to bother with 'that sort of thing'! My clearest memory of the English version of *The Hellfire Club* is that had it starred Bill and Ben The Flowerpot Men it couldn't have engendered fewer complaints from Mrs Whitehouse's predecessors. Every part of the female anatomy, suggestive or otherwise, was covered – with one exception, the navel. Which leads me to digress briefly: I once played in a TV drama, *The Last Word on Julia* with Sue Lloyd, in which I had to place a jewel in her navel. The purpose escapes me – well, it would, wouldn't it? But it entailed three shots, including a close-up. I thought it necessary to make a detailed study of this word 'navel' and looked it up. I quote: 'Belly depression left by the abruption of the umbilical cord.' That lovely lady must forgive me when I say that I found her navel, unfluffy though it was, about as sexually attractive as the *Oxford English Dictionary*'s description. A navel is a navel, is a navel – male or female!

We also shot a Japanese version of *The Hellfire Club*, the differences being mainly, of course, in an orgy scene. For the English version it was necessary to cover four female parts, but for the Japanese who have a tendency to let it all hang out a little, it was just the one. There was a scene involving a sword fight where I found myself lying across the lap of a young lady, who leant over me and smiled. She was a well-built girl, as I remember, and when the assistant director yelled, 'All right, girls, Japanese!' there was a pause as they disrobed and suddenly I saw this girl in all her glory, well most of it, and I remember thinking, 'Keep your eyes closed, particularly during the close-up!'

The Hellfire Club was in the sixties; in the seventies, by way of contrast, I took up playing pantomime. In all my years of doing so it was always my ambition to perform a traditional comedy routine, one with all the 'business' and gags. The best place for this is the 'Kitchen Scene', where most of the props required can legitimately be found to hand. And what props! I remember, as a child, watching the Dame making a stew with the most outrageous ingredients – an old boot, a tin of liver salts with the tin thrown in; then she made dumplings with flour and water so Jack, who was helping, got an extra bath – as did several people in the front row, then she pretended to throw those dumplings at us children, but they turned out to be made of cotton wool with a sweet inside. I once played with Reg Dixon, a comedian with years of pantomime experience, and I asked him if he would explain the mechanics of that particular routine, which of course he knew well. He kindly agreed and although I made copious notes I came to the conclusion that this routine, like countless others he could have performed in his sleep, was almost impossible to get across in technical terms.

My most enjoyable panto was my first, in 1977, with my dear departed friend, Dickie Henderson, in *Cinderella* at Bromley. He was such a pro and I learned so much from working with him that was to stand me in such good stead for the next panto years that followed. I played Baron Hardup to his Buttons, which I imagined was a juvenile role. But I was taken to task for thinking this by another mate, Billy Dainty, a superb pantomime Dame. It was backstage at the Victoria Palace during a Command Performance that he expounded the theory, much to my bewilderment, that it would have been quite in order for me, then aged sixty-six, with the advantage of my still slight physique, to have played Buttons. Cinderella is treated like a servant by everyone so she seeks a friend, a father figure, which role Buttons fills, and it is only while the plot is being resolved, that Buttons, still the clown – the comic the audience has been laughing at – momentarily drops the mask to reveal his love for her. So who was I to argue with Billy, he knew it all! But it was a risk I would never take.

A complaint by comics that seems to arise annually when they appear in pantomime is that of too much time being given to singing – and I have to plead guilty, I'm afraid. John Inman, who you will no doubt remember from the TV series *Are You Being Served?*, happens to be a great panto Ugly Sister and told me one day of an experience he had when playing in *Cinderella*. It seems this rather dismal young lady preceded John's main comedy spot, wailing her way through some awful pop song, making it very difficult for him to follow. Having suffered this for a week, he called the company manager and insisted that her number be cut. Such decisions are respectfully referred to the theatre manager who in this case rushed round to John's dressing room where, almost on bended knee, he pleaded, 'Mr Inman, I implore you, don't cut that song. I sell more ice-cream during that number than I do during the entire interval!'

For the most part, I fear true pantomime has gone. The talented artists, old-stagers, have been replaced far too often by so-called personalities, some more at home in, say, the sports arena than in front of the footlights. Even so, panto, whatever its pedigree, remains very important to provincial theatre, particularly at a time of cuts in local grants due to government restrictions. Pantomime is the annual insurance against the vicissitudes that can befall so much endeavour and hard work involved in keeping a theatre open.

14

The Final Clutter

I have a feeling that my wife senses the end of this book is nigh, that the final chapter of these cluttered reminiscences has begun and soon she will be able to enjoy the pleasure of my company for an evening's television (this is, of course, conjecture on my part). However, she has, as a possible inducement, just presented me with the video of *JFK*, one of my favourite films. The process of American democracy, its politics and corruption has always intrigued me, particularly when it involves the assassination of one of its Presidents. It also has a rather obscure but nevertheless personal significance concerning the time when Nina and I had sought refuge from the matrimonial storm, staying at Jack Grossman's flat. Most people seem to be able to recall what they were doing when the assassination was suddenly announced on the radio. Nina had gone to bed after a tiring day, and Kathie, who was also staying at the flat, and I were washing up after the endless communal evening meal, for which there was a rota. Having heard the news we both stood numbed and almost disbelieving. Kathie mumbled something through her tears and I went on endlessly drying the same cup. Finally we discussed the question of whether to wake the others, feeling almost that we couldn't bear the burden alone; instead we had a cup of tea, in total silence. As I remember that was the only dark cloud during our entire stay with the Grossmans.

*

During my later years I have kept a short list of roles that I really wanted to play and it didn't matter where, or even how, as long as the opportunity came before I was too old and had to pass them by – such as Willy Loman in *Death of a Salesman*; Schweik in Hasek's *The Good Soldier Schweik*; Alfie again, but this time on the stage, and there are others; among them was Doolittle in George Bernard Shaw's *Pygmalion*. So I took the part in the Yvonne Arnaud Theatre's production of *Pygmalion*. I was fully aware of the reverence in which Wilfrid Lawson was held for his interpretation of the role – elderly actors almost genuflected when recalling his performance as Doolittle. I had never had the good fortune to witness his apparently superb stage characterization and in spite of my desire to play the role, I developed something of a complex seeing the adulation accorded to Mr Lawson.

That is, until I saw the 1938 film in which he re-created his masterpiece. I found it amazing. Amazing because it was beyond my comprehension how anyone could arrive at such a concept of Doolittle's character. Shaw's dustman has a total lack of respect for his betters and he's not afraid to let Higgins know that although he is prepared to play 'their game', it will be on his terms. It's a gift of a part, a cabaret. Of course, a little social understanding helps. I achieved everything I wanted from him. As a Birmingham critic wrote, 'Bernard Shaw would have been proud'. But there were others who were unimpressed, as I discovered in Bradford when leaving the theatre after a performance. I was confronted by a group of disappointed customers who complained vehemently: 'Where were the songs?' 'What about "I Could Have Danced All Night"?' Well, I mean, what can one say?

Returning home, one day, from filming, I was met, almost on the doorstep, by Kathie insisting that I see the new play by Trevor Griffiths which had just opened in the West End. It was called *Comedians* and there was a wonderful part in it that she felt should go on my 'list'. She even paid for the seats to prove her point! The part – that of Eddie Waters, a respected popular comedian now retired, who runs evening classes for would-be comics – was a gift. It was played by my old friend Jimmy Jewel, whose interpretation of the role, I have to confess, I totally disagreed with – as I have told Richard Eyre, the director, on several occasions. Eddie Waters is a man inspired, he will have none of his pupils' cynicism, he believes entirely in what he's doing. He must! Why else would he bother with these dumb-bells? Only the arrogant Gethin Price appears to have sufficient intelligence to understand what Eddie is trying to do. As usual, Kathie was right, *Comedians* went to the top of my list of 'parts to play'. And, as luck would have it, an offer to play the part came eventually, in 1977, but from a most unusual source. I had a call from Hugh Cruttwell, the Principal of the Royal Academy of Dramatic Art, who explained the students' choice of *Comedians* as their end-of-term performance had presented problems regarding the age and character of Eddie Waters, adding that he also felt the students would benefit enormously from working with an established actor so, in view of the difficulty, would I consider accepting the role? He also pointed out that this was the first time in the history of the Academy that such a thing had happened, and, to my knowledge, it remains some kind of record.

I must admit at first to having doubts, these were not the circumstances I'd envisaged for my début as Eddie Waters. I had no idea what the general standard of acting was among the students at RADA – some of them might have won medals for their Shakespearean performances, but it wasn't going to help them play a North Country club comic! Nevertheless, there was this nagging doubt that this might become another coveted part that would have to be deleted from the shortlist due to lack of other offers. Having explained my reasons for playing the role and on the understanding that the director, Richard Digby Day, would accept my interpretation in his production of the play, I said I would accept. They agreed.

Came the day when the cast gathered together for the first

time – the excitement, the expectancy! But quite frankly, I didn't know what to expect. So I met them, they were cordial but canny, respectful but not reverential, thank heavens! I soon learned that they were perfectly aware of the uncertainties of this so-called profession they had chosen, but they were young and laughed them away. I levelled with them from the start – no condescension, I ate with them in the canteen, I drank with them in the pub, but in rehearsal I gave no quarter, and they expected none. We got along fine.

The four performances were a riot, the enthusiasm of those student audiences just made me 'take off', and despite the euphoria, I proved to myself that my concept of Eddie Waters was best for the play. But none of it seemed to matter any more, it was the five weeks I spent with those young actors, being one of them, catching their enthusiasm for the future, which made it for me one of my most memorable experiences. After the last performance, the students presented me with a magnificent pipe, a touching and amusing gesture on their part, amusing because, as Eddie, I'd refused to bother with one in the play. Thanking them afterwards, I remember saying to one young man, 'You may have to begin carrying a spear!' Actually, he didn't. His name was Anton Lesser and, within a short time, he became a leading player with the Royal Shakespeare Company.

Just recently I was very pleased to receive a phone call from the Leader of the National Youth Orchestra asking my permission, as lyricist, for the orchestra to record one of the many songs I wrote with Mike Sammes, called 'It's So Easy'.

My partnership with Mike, as song writers, has existed over many years, during which our output has been moderate but varied. The extraordinary thing about our partnership is that in over twenty years of collaboration we have met but once, and then for a brief moment when he delivered a song to my flat in Marylebone High Street. The usual routine would be that I posted him a lyric which he would then set to music, making any slight alteration necessary. He would then send me a copy of the completed song for my file and that was that. Not once did we find it necessary to meet in order to discuss the work in hand or each other's contribution. This, I concluded, must be due to some kind of mental telepathy between us, which will no doubt come as a surprise to Mike. But he will appreciate that a lyricist will work with some kind of musical pattern in mind when putting the words together. The other extraordinary thing is that the tune which he composes later invariably loosely follows the melodic pattern previously used by myself when arriving at the lyrics. In the case of 'It's So Easy' it proved to be note for note! But with a track record of nearly eighty recorded songs, why was I so excited about this one? I think because it came from the young 'uns – the National Youth Orchestra. Just as I enjoyed working with the student actors, I liked the thought of doing something for student musicians – an extension, perhaps, to my interest in working for the Boys' Clubs.

But let us digress and speak of the 'magic of the theatre', of 'the show must go on' and 'there's no business like show business' and all the other crap including 'the show's the thing' (to paraphrase William S). It most certainly isn't when, after all the sweat, blood, toil and tears of the rehearsals prior to opening night, the nearest one can find to a complimentary notice in the following morning's press is: 'Added to the diffusiveness of his many themes was the contracting of bladder cancer, which surely must be quite the most unpromising topic for a play in a long time.' Such was the general consensus of critical opinion when Peter Ransley's play, *Runaway*, opened at the Royal Court Theatre in March 1974. But 'the show must go on' and it was with something akin to dread that I approached the stage door for the second night, knowing full well that my fellow actors and I were about to suffer the horror of our voices echoing around the auditorium. Then some bright spark in the publicity department came up with a brilliant idea – well, he thought so!

It was the week following the play's opening that a headline on the *Evening Standard* announced – 'See Royal Court play for just 1p!' and continued:

> The Royal Court has scrapped its fixed price on tickets and introduced a make-us-an-offer system for the rest of the run of its current production. Theatre-goers wanting to see Peter Ransley's play *Runaway* now at the Court, will be invited to name their own price for tickets – down to 1p if they choose. Mr Oscar Lewenstein, artistic director of the Court, today explained why the system had been introduced. He said, 'We are not getting a large audience for *Runaway* and we believe it is a play that deserves to be seen. It was only scheduled for a four-week run and it takes longer than that for word-of-mouth to get around.

As I remember, this gimmick had little or no effect at the box office; as should be expected, it might even have become a joke: a regular in the pub next door to the Court asked me 'How's the penny gaff going?'

It was late summer, 1988, when I had a call from Lindsay Anderson, which was most unusual, for as a rule we kept in touch by sending picture postcards when we were away from home, his coming from as far as Moscow and mine rarely further away than Huddersfield. He told me that David Storey had written a new play called *The March on Russia* which he, Lindsay, would direct. It was to be presented at the National in the Lyttelton Theatre, and I would be sent a script to consider the part of a character called Passmore. The play concerns the gathering of the Passmore family, two daughters and a son, played, respectively, by Rosemary Martin, Patsy Rowlands and Frank Grimes, to celebrate the birthday of their mother, played by Constance Chapman. Once again, skeletons emerge from the cupboard, including the relationships between old Tommy Passmore and his wife after sixty years of marriage. It has all the ingredients for a family tragedy, but because of David's skill as a writer, it is also an extremely funny play for a great deal of the time. The scenes between Mr and Mrs Passmore, whose only means of communication after a lifetime's relationship is through badinage and insult, becomes quite hilarious at times. I was being offered the prize of a lifetime when it's normally too late to look for prizes. This was the greatest part I've ever been offered, with the chance to prove I could still do it after all these years.

We opened at the Lyttelton Theatre on Friday 7 April 1989 to great acclaim and some of the best notices I have ever received. I have them before me, all stuck in the album, which remains open for further offers! But if they are slow in coming, or even if they don't come at all, I shall come up here, to my little eyrie and, although strictly it 'shouldn't be done', I'll read them once again, just to remind myself I *can* still do it.

'You win some, you lose some,' the saying goes. The 1993 television production of John Osborne's *The Entertainer* was not such a great triumph. I had been present at the world première of the play at the Royal Court Theatre on 10 April 1957, with its star-studded cast, and audience. The players included Dorothy Tutin as Jean Rice, Brenda de Banzie as Queenie, George Ralph as Billy, and Laurence Olivier giving one of the greatest performances of his illustrious career as Archie.

Edith and I, making our way back to our seats after the interval, were hailed by a young Peter Brook with: 'This is one for you, Bill!' But as the final curtain fell I knew that this was a part I would never attempt. There have been offers from theatrical companies around the country, but I have always backed off. When asked, the reasons I give for such an attitude are often dismissed as having no foundation. So I will be brief. It takes a tragic actor, not a comic one, to play the part of the entertainer, Archie Rice, for he is a total failure as a stand-up comic. The story goes that when asked how he was able to act such a bad comic, Olivier replied, 'I did my best.' Archie's real tragedy is his awareness of his failure as a son, husband, father, entertainer and even as an ex-public schoolboy. That veneer, that particular public charm – which he should not have tried to act – had failed him. Now, whilst John Osborne himself may also reject my thesis, let me say I once saw Max Wall attempt Archie Rice and, for me, the result was ludicrous. Here was one of the country's most brilliant comics trying to act a bad one, with the personal tragedy of Archie replaced by a kind of melancholia. As the *Daily Telegraph* said, '... Max Wall's very competence is a handicap. His Archie gets genuine laughs when the effect of the play demands that its jokes should fall flat. There is grace in Mr Wall's agile movements where there should be clumsiness: there is total hostility in his face, but no miserable sense of total failure.'

However, I must confess to mixed feelings on my return to TV drama as Billy Rice, with Michael Gambon as Archie. It had been so long, and working practices had changed, some of which of course I had become aware of over the years with *Summer Wine*. For example, today there is the seemingly growing avoidance among the film crews of even reasonable complaint or compromise. It's like a re-awakening of the thirties; forever living with the ghost of unemployment – 'If you don't want the job, there's plenty out there that do.' The final threat, the dole queue. My father knew it, so did I. Is this the legacy I must leave my grandsons? But, back to Billy Rice. We rehearsed the play for three or four weeks, then retired to the studios for a week's recordings. Perhaps retired is hardly the description, we worked, with the usual breaks, from 10 a.m. until 10 p.m. But advantages were taken, working on one occasion as late as midnight.

The TV showing of *The Entertainer* was brought forward to early December in order to avoid the usual glut of Yuletide 'entertainment'. The date however clashed with an invitation to some pre-Christmas festivities, and what's more, a couple of days prior to that we had been 'turned over', to use that soft-option colloquialism, losing, among other things, our telly and video recorder. Friends came to the rescue and recorded it for us, but the press were hardly jubilant and Kathie, knowing of my doubts during rehearsals, diplomatically declined to suggest we take a look for ourselves. But, come Boxing Day and family gathered, I could resist no longer. I was very disappointed.

As I reflect, it was not until I was approaching the age of seventy that I began to realize that life was settling down, but the question was would I ever settle for it? To this day the question remains unanswered. Nevertheless, generally, with my renewed involvement in social issues and politics I knew where I was at and the people with whom I was associated. I had become actively involved, as I am today, as a Vice-President, Executive Member and Arts Adviser to the London Federation of Boys' Clubs. I also accepted the Chair of Unity Theatre Trust, I became involved with Pensioners' Rights, led by Jack Jones, and travelled the country during general elections. But I suppose my greatest achievement came as founder member of Arts for Labour, taking the Chair at its inception and retiring in 1993 when I became its President.

> Arts for Labour is an association of Labour Party supporters interested in the arts either as professionals or constituency party members, MPs, and others interested in establishing a permanent arts policy. A policy to improve and sustain our culture as a means of enjoyment, entertainment and education, free from the wiles and whims of a corporate society and government.

These are bold words and, I must hasten to add, my own, but they were the basis of my discussion with Tony Benn, whose opinion I had sought. His reaction was very favourable and as a result I met Jim Mortimer, the then General Secretary, who welcomed the idea. So it was at a reception in the House of Commons, attended by many celebrities, that Arts for Labour was launched by the then Leader of the Opposition, Michael Foot.

But for all the protestations of returning to my roots, my renewed vision of existence and a life of good causes, there is one important factor I have failed to mention. It is that, now into my eighties, and ironically for the first time, I can claim personal financial security.

People sometimes ask me if I wished this success had come earlier. Patience permitting, I point out that I have already tasted the good life, the rich living, but could hardly claim it as always due to my own personal financial independence. I also reflect on the fact that if it had not been for *Summer Wine*, I might have been just another aged actor, sitting alone, forgotten, and knowing it. But I am not forgotten, I'm even spoilt a little, accorded a certain respect, even – and I'm still working! In other words, I like it the way it is. Any ambitions left? To write a really good play and live to see it performed.

I do have one last admission, which is that during the writing of these final chapters I took what I can only describe as a kind of sick leave. In other words, I became sick and tired of this mini-saga of mine. One does – the introspection, the turning back of the years, not always with satisfaction and often with regret, so I went for long walks in Highgate Woods, meddled in the garden, and still found I couldn't shake off this malaise, particularly when the weather was wet, cold and uncomfortable. Deep down in my wellies I knew I had to turn to something else, write about something or someone else. So, after I'd mooned about and got underfoot, Kathie suggested I re-read *The Fruits of Philosophy*. This was a play with the legal-sounding subtitle, *The Queen v Bradlaugh and Besant on a Charge of Obscenity*. The title *Fruits of Philosophy* was the name of a pamphlet published forty years earlier by an American, Dr Knowlten, which was mainly concerned with the female productive organism and conception, giving advice regarding the prevention of large families among the poor. Although it had been successfully prosecuted a year earlier in 1876, Charles Bradlaugh and Annie Besant saw fit to re-publish it and were duly brought to stand trial at the Guildhall on 8 June 1877, the proceedings lasting four days.

Having researched the trial thoroughly, it became the main theme of my play with a sub-plot which did little more than illustrate and laud Annie's efforts and courage on behalf of London's poor. I submitted it to Granada TV for a series they were putting together on the lives of notable Victorian women, only to have it rejected with the explanation that they already had a play concerning this trial.

The subject of Victorian London's East End, particularly that of the Matchgirls and Annie Besant has been with me for more than half a century and I still write of that period. Only a few years ago Macmillan Educational published another play of mine, *These Boots Ain't Made for Walking*, again concerning the match workers of Bryant and May. This dealt with the subject of a Bill by Mr Robert Lowe proposing a tax of a halfpenny on each box of matches. Whilst no doubt smiled upon by the directors, it led to a spontaneous reaction by their employees. Processions were organized, mainly by the women workers.

Having written four plays in which Annie Besant has played a major role, I think I can claim that my researching has led me to reading just about every book published on that woman's life. Such familiarity with the subject inevitably brought many varied opinions to my notice which led to my idol-worship being gradually replaced by further questioning and doubt. The seed may have been sown unconsciously years before when in conversation with Malcolm Muggeridge. He and his wife had a weekend flat above ours in Brighton and I was extolling the virtues of the lady in question only to be shattered by his reaction, which was totally derisive.

So when I took down from my shelves, some twenty-five years later, *The Fruits of Philosophy*, I knew it was the trial that would become the background or sub-plot. I had to write a new play about Annie, examining the varied opinions, the gossip, the scandal, and above all finding the answers to my questions in doing so. Furthermore, had these questions existed at the time and if they did, did they matter as far as she was concerned?

When, finally, it was staged I was slightly perturbed at the first-night audience's seeming non-reaction, even to my rare attempts at humour. Since there was no interval I eventually succumbed to a deep depression, convinced they had all fallen asleep. Then, to my complete surprise, there was loud and enthusiastic applause as the curtain fell, and we finished the short run to full houses. The reason for the apparently somnolent audience was their straining endeavours to hear against the noise of the passing traffic. The theatre is a converted pub with no insulation, situated on a main thoroughfare.

I was, therefore, sufficiently satisfied and returned to the drawing board to work further on the play, paying attention to Annie's great work in India, her relationship with Ghandi and some new, and surprising, developments with theosophy. I changed the title to *A Change of Vestments* and submitted it to my literary agent as a play for radio. Whatever happens to it, at least I shall have got it off my chest.

Thinking of Annie Besant reminds me of *Matchgirls* and of musicals in general which leads me to 'the one that got away'. Its subject was to have been Josephine Baker, born of black parents in St Louis and suffering the usual poverty and indignity of the Southern States. At a very early age she discovered she had the ability to make folk laugh, a talent, nevertheless, she must have been hard put to use, given her surroundings. So she took off for the illusory world of showbiz. At the age of twelve she joined the 'Chocolate Dandies', a cheap vaudeville show, as a chorus dancer, touring the coloured circuit. And as chorus dancers go, she didn't! Eccentric dancer is more accurate since she pulled funny faces at her audience – but they laughed and she was given a solo spot. Several years later she travelled to France with a show and her fate was sealed, but only after a shaky start when she was welcomed by a smiling docker with '*Bonjour, ma cocotte.*' She smiled back, later to be annoyed when she discovered the literal translation to be 'Good day, my black stewing pot'! But French was to become her adopted tongue and she would learn that *cocotte* is a term of endearment – the docker was paying her a compliment. Paris followed suit, taking her to its heart and she became the toast of the town, star of the Folies, the Casino and the Lido. There she gave up pulling faces, set aside her eccentric dancing and became an elegant chanteuse – with or without clothes.

I was first drawn to her story by the fact that she had received the Medal of Resistance given by General de Gaulle for her work as an undercover agent. Then there was Les Milandes, a castle purchased by her and her husband, the dance-band leader Jo Bouillon, which was to become the home of 'The Rainbow Tribe'. This was a group of eight or nine babies of different nationalities adopted by them from around the world.

This surely had all the elements of a great musical story – poor girl – and black at that – makes good, becomes a big star, a war heroine and finally conceives the wonderful idea of an infant United Nations! So countless notes and observations were made regarding a story-line and general format for the show. I ended up with a bulging file of information which sat on my desk as I spasmodically arranged to visit a friend in Paris who would arrange a meeting with Josephine. But it became one of those things that one never quite gets around to doing, something always seemed to crop up ... well, that's maybe an excuse. The real reason may have been an early and logical observation by my son: 'But Dad, how many people in this country have ever heard of Josephine Baker, never mind seen her? It would be like expecting the French to go wild over *The Vera Lynn Story*.'

My enthusiasm returned with the announcement of her

farewell performance at the London Palladium. I rang Billy
Marsh of London Management who was very keen on my
idea of a musical and I asked him to use his influence for me
to see her after the show. The theatre was not full, but the
audience was enthusiastic and there was a buzz of anticipation
in the air. She was over sixty-five now, surely they weren't
expecting her legendary songs and dances, wearing an almost
non-existent costume. But let's face it, for me this lady was
just so much documented research and press cuttings. I'd
never seen her before in my life. But there was no need to
worry because other than the costume she had on for her
first appearance, mainly feathers worn over a body stocking,
there were no surprises, it was to be an evening dedicated
to a long-gone past. She sang, told stories and the audience
joined in the choruses. Obviously she was reviving a lot of
memories.

But it meant little to me, it was an evening for aficionados,
the nostalgia was too early and it was all a little sad. She saw
Kathie and me after the show, but she was obviously tired. I
briefly told her the object of my visit, that of asking her
permission to write a story-line for a musical production of
her life. She told me that negotiations were already under way
in Paris for a show and I suggested that should they fall
through, perhaps I could visit her in France where we might
discuss the project further. She agreed and we took our leave.
A few months later I read that the Paris negotiations had
fallen through, but I never got in touch with her again. She
died on 12 April 1975.

In late October 1993 the 'coming of age' of *Last of the Summer
Wine* was duly celebrated by an excellent press, four important
national newspapers, each contributing a half-page spread.
Insignificant as they may be amidst all the shameful events in
this world today, I want to record them for posterity!

'It's always sunny, even when they're all wrapped up against
the wind. Nobody is hurt when they fall and nobody dies. It's

about an old age that never ages. No wonder we love it so,' Stephen Gilbert wrote in the *Independent*.

'A vintage comedy-brew twenty years on! Already the longest-running situation comedy in the world, can *Last of the Summer Wine* keep going for another twenty-one years? Compo replies, "I wouldn't count on it, but Roy Clarke may have to write us into bathchairs soon!"' wrote Andrew Preston of the *Daily Express*. And in *The Times* Roy Hattersley wrote: 'When the broadcast ends with the three sprites, Compo, Clegg and Foggy, looking across the limestone landscape of Yorkshire, recall that you are supposed to sigh for the lost innocence they represent. And enjoy one of the funniest series ever to appear on television.'

While in the *Observer* Andy Midhurst wrote: '*Last of the Summer Wine* is time-warp television, a pictorial nostalgia fantasy with an almost bravura disdain for the complications of contemporary life. It can keep running forever because it was never set in the present in the first place! Perfectly scheduled after *Songs of Praise*, *Last of the Summer Wine* offers a thirty-minute haven, a very English repudiation of the here and now, with a frighteningly well-proved emotional pull. If John Major wants to get the country back to basics, then the party political broadcast has already been made and it goes out this evening at seven o'clock!'

Already booked for a further series, I have reached my eighties, and perfect strangers will still continue to nod and smile, whether I'm in Brighton or Budleigh Salterton, but I'll be looking forward to getting back to Yorkshire because it's home, you see. I know I'll be welcomed off the train by friends and staff alike at Wakefield – Eric will be waiting with the car to take me to my delightful bungalow where Ruby and Harry wait to tend my every need. Still in the spotlight after fifty-seven years when I first became an entertainer at Dovercourt Holiday Camp. Someone up there must be looking after me!

*

I have been with this 'clutter' long enough now, my wellies are back in the woodshed, and the garden looks better for my absence. So I call a halt to these ramblings of mine, hoping they will find their way into a volume which at some time in the future may be discovered in a dusty loft, waiting to fall into the hands of a reader keen to know more, but saddened that their generation never savoured the unique bouquet of *Last of the Summer Wine*.

By way of an epilogue I have chosen a poem written to celebrate my seventieth birthday. It is by a fine writer and poet and good friend of mine. We shared a similar childhood background and, for me, the poem turns back those faded photograph years. W4 is the postal code for Acton Green, where I was born.

W4

And tho' the voices are stilled
and nothing moves that fetched
you running, Bill, the houses remain;
solid Victorian homes reflecting all
the values that made you.

But the sprauncy lads, West End styled,
all dolled up and nowhere to go,
have gone at last, unless you watch
at some dim hour for a stubborn shade,
slipped across Chiswick Common
in vain pursuit of a time forgotten girl,
now a Granny, vaguely remembered by you
from the Hammersmith Palais.

The iron gate at number three
still groans from ailing hinges.
But no Mother stands, arms folded,
waiting for the deciding marble to be tossed
(Just *five* more minutes, Mum?)
and argued over until it's as late as seven,
but not yet time for Dad to appear.
And he won't, for we are all his age, Bill,
our roles reversed.

But I know you feel the alternate
blinding, brightness and flickering shadows
of the paling fence, warm wooded from
a low summer sun as you walk home,
your actor's senses alert for just one cry,
one shout from a mate appeared suddenly.

Harry Lovelock, March, 1983